T0312318

Cambridge Elements ≡

Elements in Intercultural Communication
edited by
Will Baker
University of Southampton
Troy McConachy
University of Warwick
Sonia Morán Panero
University of Southampton

INTERCULTURAL COMMUNICATION AND IDENTITY

Ron Darvin
The University of British Columbia
Tongle Sun
The Chinese University of Hong Kong

CAMBRIDGE
UNIVERSITY PRESS

Shaftesbury Road, Cambridge CB2 8EA, United Kingdom

One Liberty Plaza, 20th Floor, New York, NY 10006, USA

477 Williamstown Road, Port Melbourne, VIC 3207, Australia

314–321, 3rd Floor, Plot 3, Splendor Forum, Jasola District Centre, New Delhi – 110025, India

103 Penang Road, #05–06/07, Visioncrest Commercial, Singapore 238467

Cambridge University Press is part of Cambridge University Press & Assessment, a department of the University of Cambridge.

We share the University's mission to contribute to society through the pursuit of education, learning and research at the highest international levels of excellence.

www.cambridge.org
Information on this title: www.cambridge.org/9781009478571

DOI: 10.1017/9781009206754

First published 2024

A catalogue record for this publication is available from the British Library.

ISBN 978-1-009-47857-1 Hardback
ISBN 978-1-009-20673-0 Paperback
ISSN 2752-5589 (online)
ISSN 2752-5570 (print)

Cambridge University Press & Assessment has no responsibility for the persistence or accuracy of URLs for external or third-party internet websites referred to in this publication and does not guarantee that any content on such websites is, or will remain, accurate or appropriate.

Intercultural Communication and Identity

Elements in Intercultural Communication

DOI: 10.1017/9781009206754
First published online: January 2024

Ron Darvin
The University of British Columbia

Tongle Sun
The Chinese University of Hong Kong

Author for correspondence: Ron Darvin, ron.darvin@ubc.ca

Abstract: This Element asserts how identity as a construct enables a critical awareness of how speakers position themselves and are positioned by others in intercultural encounters. It discusses how identity vis-à-vis culture has been theorized through social psychological, poststructuralist, and critical lenses, and how identity is discursively constructed and mediated. Rejecting essentialist notions of language and culture, this Element demonstrates how inscriptions of identity such as race, ethnicity, nationality, and class can be used to critically examine the dynamics of situated intercultural encounters and to understand how such interactions can index competing and colluding ideologies. By examining identity research from different parts of the world, it casts a light on how identities are performed in diverse intercultural contexts and discusses research methodologies that have been employed to examine identity in intercultural communication.

Keywords: identity, ideology, positionality, inequality, critical intercultural communication

ISBNs: 9781009478571 (HB), 9781009206730 (PB), 9781009206754 (OC)
ISSNs: 2752-5589 (online), 2752-5570 (print)

Contents

1 Introduction

As a fundamental construct in the field of language and intercultural communication, identity provides a lens through which to understand the way we position ourselves and are positioned by others during interaction. Our sense of self, our subjectivity, is constructed through language (Weedon, 1987), and we perform identities in different intercultural contexts by deploying our linguistic and semiotic resources and negotiating affiliations and ascriptions of identity such as race, ethnicity, nationality, and social class (Block, 2012). Whether we are learning a second language, migrating to another country, studying abroad, working in multicultural contexts, or interacting online, intercultural communication takes place in increasingly diverse forms and contexts. In this globalized world, the transnational flow of capital, goods, people, and ideas (Appadurai, 1990), together with advancements in technology, have contributed to new modes of interaction, allegiances, and notions of citizenship. Identities have become unbounded and deterritorialized, no longer tied to fixed localities, patterns, or cultural traditions, transforming life strategies while exerting new demands on the self (Elliott & Urry, 2010). As people traverse the local and the global and the online and the offline with greater fluidity, they shift identities in complex ways as they interact with diverse others. The paradox of globalization, however, is that while the interconnectedness of the world has become more apparent, particularly with the immediacy and simultaneity of news and social media, the world has also become increasingly fragmented and polarized. Power operates in these changing contexts and networks in often concealed ways, ushering people into isolated spaces while constructing new forms of inequality and modes of othering (Holliday, 2010).

While our sense of place in the social world shifts across time and space, certain identities can also be assumed or imposed on us (Pavlenko & Blackledge, 2004) with a certain degree of fixedness, and as we negotiate these different positionalities, identity becomes a site of struggle: dynamic, multiple, and oftentimes contradictory (Norton, 2013). Understood from this poststructuralist perspective, identity contributes to a critical understanding of intercultural communication by resisting essentialist notions of culture and recognizing the intersectionality of social categories. Past theories of cultural identity tended to uphold the notion of cultures as geographically and nationally distinct entities and presupposing that "a world of human differences is to be conceptualized as a diversity of separate societies, each with its own culture" (Gupta & Ferguson, 1997, p. 1). In recent years, what constitutes "culture" has become more difficult to apprehend and some identity scholars have drawn attention to how the attribution of qualities to specific groups of people can essentialize and reify identities in ways that do not account for changing contexts and situations (Atkinson, 1999). More than regarding culture as a product, something shared by groups of people, it has been understood as discourse and as practice (Baker, 2015), and that while there are ways of communicating that can be attributed to culture, not all issues of intercultural interactions are necessarily about cultural differences.

By recognizing intercultural communication as a social practice (Piller, 2017), identity research challenges the structuralist view that language, culture, and nation are stable and contained elements that one can draw correlations from (Kramsch & Uryu, 2020). Instead of ascribing an essentialized cultural identity to nations and individuals, a fluid and open intercultural communication examines "how individuals, in order to achieve their communication goals, negotiate cultural or linguistic differences which may be perceived relevant by at least one party in the interaction" (Zhu, 2019, p. 210), and for Baker (2015), these parties can include either the researcher or the interlocutors themselves. This conceptualization of intercultural communication provides a way to understand the tension between recognizing the fluidity of identities and acknowledging the temporary fixedness of self-ascription. It asserts how researchers cannot make a priori assumptions of speakers in intercultural situations in terms of their race, ethnicity, or nationality, but that these inscriptions of identity do take shape when interlocutors refer to them to position themselves or others in discourse (Davies & Harré, 1990). This perspective draws attention to the micro-level of interaction and meaning making, and recognizes how identity is socially constructed in diverse situations while also negotiated within conditions that bear the mark of historical and institutional constraints.

Aligned with this view of intercultural communication as contextualized and situated (Holliday, 2010; Kramsch, 2009; Piller, 2017; Zhu, 2019), this Element draws attention to how identity is constructed, mediated, and negotiated within contexts of difference and power. Operating within the tensions of structure and agency (Block, 2013), it is constituted not only by language but also by systems of thought and their symbolic power (Kramsch, 2009). These ideologies shape dispositions, beliefs, and practices, including the way we position ourselves and others in intercultural encounters. To introduce this notion of identity, this Element traces the history in which this pivotal construct has been theorized in applied linguistics, from social psychological, poststructural, and critical perspectives, and discusses how it has been researched in diverse intercultural contexts using different methodologies. It draws on studies that have either been framed explicitly as intercultural communication research or that involve communication in intercultural contexts and situations. Weaving all these ideas together, the Element concludes by describing contemporary challenges in identity research and suggesting future directions.

2 Theorizing Identity

In applied linguistics research, different terms have been associated with identity: "self," "role," "subjectivity," "subject position," and "agent," and while they may refer to the same object of study, they represent different theoretical perspectives and foreground specific ideas. The self, for instance, is regarded as a psychological entity, and self-concept refers to the cognitive and affective dimensions that shape what we believe about ourselves (Mercer, 2011). Subjectivity, on the other hand, is a poststructuralist term that refers to the conscious or unconscious self produced through discourse, that is, how we are "formed as subjects through the symbols we create, the chains of signification we construct and the meanings we exchange with others" (Kramsch, 2014, p. 215). Subject position foregrounds how speakers position themselves in discourse in interaction with others (Kramsch, 2009), while agent, from a sociocultural perspective, highlights how individuals can be shaped but not completely determined by context and have the capacity for self-determination.

2.1 Social Psychological Perspectives of Identity

Scholars in the 1970s and 1980s interested in identity research tended to draw distinctions between social identity and cultural identity. Advancing a social identity theory that highlighted the dichotomy between in-group and out-group, Tajfel (1982) referred to social identity as the relationship between individuals and the larger social world, mediated through institutions like families, schools, workplaces, social services, and law courts (e.g., Gumperz, 1982). Cultural identity, on the other hand, referred to the relationship between an individual and members of a particular ethnic group who share a common history and language, as well as similar ways of understanding the world. Drawing on Tajfel's (1982) conception of social identity that highlighted how people categorize the social world and perceive themselves as members of groups, Giles and Johnson (1987) theorized how ethnolinguistic identity and solidarity shaped predispositions toward speech accommodation and language maintenance, and how in both conceptions identities are constituted through differentiation of specific traits or values. Identity categories of race, gender, or nationality served as independent variables where speakers were classified according to their membership of different social groups, and certain correlations or causal relations were investigated between these groups and certain qualities, behaviors, or attitudes.

Questions regarding identity were tied to notions of culture or community and shared history, language, or geographical region.

Social psychology research has also understood identity in terms of the way people define themselves in part by their membership of social groups. In this sense, belonging is both initiated and sustained: a knowledge of group membership and an emotional attachment to this belonging, and where such membership has a causal relationship in terms of actions and behaviour (Benwell & Stokoe, 2006). In language learning research, developing competence in another language meant being able to identify with a target second-language (L2) community and taking on aspects of their behavior (Gardner & Lambert, 1972). Recognizing the significance of individual differences and the thoughts and motives of the self, Dörnyei (2009) theorized the notion of the ideal self and the ought-to self to refer to the attributes a learner would like to possess and believes they should possess. For Mercer (2011), it is the unique set of self-beliefs of individuals that influences their choices and actions, helping them make sense of their position in the world.

2.2 Poststructuralist Perspectives of Identity

Resisting notions of a fixed and coherent core of an individual, poststructuralist perspectives of identity recognize that individuals construct *subjectivities* (Weedon, 1987), "the conscious and unconscious thoughts and emotions of the individual, her sense of herself, and her ways of understanding her relation to the world" (p. 28). These subjectivities are produced through language in ways that are always situated, dynamic, and variable. While social constructionism (Burr, 2015) highlights how identity is constructed through interaction in specific environments, poststructuralism emphasizes how such construction occurs in discourse. Mediated through symbolic forms, constituted and shaped in interaction, subjectivity is always in process as it responds to and interprets the discourse of others (Kramsch, 2009). Identities, on the other hand, are "points of temporary attachments to the subject positions which discursive practices construct for us" (Hall, 1996, p. 6). While subjectivities are emergent and ongoing, identity suggests a certain permanence or fixedness (Block, 2022). For Weedon (2004), it is the "limited and temporary fixing for the individual of a particular mode of subjectivity as apparently what one *is*" (p. 19; emphasis in the original). While one can be a subject without identification, identity involves a degree of self-recognition together with an understanding of what one is not. It foregrounds how selves are constructed in practice, that is, individuals produce, enact, or perform identities (Blommaert, 2005; Butler, 1990; Hall & Bucholtz, 1995; Wodak, 1997) as they relate or interact with others in the social world (Norton Peirce, 1995).

In her landmark study of five immigrant women in Canada from Vietnam, Peru, Poland, and the former Czechoslovakia, Bonny Norton (1995) demonstrated how the identities of these women, as immigrant, as mother, or as worker, shaped the way they understood themselves and their place in society. Conducted at a time when large-scale migration was transforming postindustrialist societies and providing more contexts for intercultural communication, this study examined how migrants occupied a variety of spaces in their country of settlement, and how acquiring a country's official language was key to social integration and meaningful employment. Native speakers of the host community, however, often served as gatekeepers to participation in different contexts by controlling access to language resources and determining rules of use. For immigrants to claim their rightful place in a new country and to imagine better futures, they had to negotiate relations at work, school, and other community settings, and assert their own identities.

In the study, Martina from Czechoslovakia would frequently refer to herself as "stupid" and "inferior" because she did not believe she was fluent enough in English:

> "I feel uncomfortable in the group of people whose English language is their mother tongue because they speak fluently without any problems and I feel inferior" (from Martina's diary, in Norton, 1995, p. 21).

However, when she had to talk to her landlord on the phone about their lease agreement, a matter that was critical to their family's finances, she mentions how she was able to go past this perceived lack of fluency and engage in a long conversation. "I got upset and I talked with him on the phone over one hour and I didn't think about the tenses rules. I had known that I couldn't give up. My children were very surprised when they heard me" (from Martina's diary, in Norton, 1995, p. 22).

Norton (1995) suggests that Martina's perseverance with speaking at that particular moment intersects with her identity as a mother responsible for the wellbeing and security of her children. During this phone conversation, she resists her feelings of inadequacy and refuses to "give up," asserting her legitimacy in this particular discourse. Understood across multiple sites of identity formation, Martina demonstrates how identity is nonunitary and contradictory, as different situations enable different subjectivities.

To draw attention to these shifting identities, Norton (2013) defines identity as "how a person understands his or her relationship to the world, how that relationship is structured across time and space, and how the person understands possibilities for the future" (p. 45). This definition highlights how it is fluid, context dependent, and context producing while shaped by various historical and material circumstances. When people speak, they not only exchange information but also reorganize "a sense of who they are and how they relate to the world" (Norton, 2013, p. 4). These contingent positions are shaped not only by lived experiences but also by imagined futures (Kanno & Norton, 2003; Norton & Pavlenko, 2019).

2.3 Critical Perspectives

While poststructuralism highlights how identity is constructed through discourse, critical perspectives associated with poststructuralism draw attention to how the discourses made available to us are themselves limited. There are dominant discourses in society that can constrain the way we perform our identities, and these discourses are constructed and reproduced through power. Pavlenko and Blackledge (2004) recognize identities as "social, discursive, and narrative options offered by a particular society in a specific time and place to which individuals and groups of individuals appeal in an attempt to self-name, to self-characterize, and to claim social spaces and social prerogatives" (p. 19). For Holland and Lave (2001), while identities are always in process, practices of identification are historically produced, shaped by broader structural forces, constituting a "history in person."

Identity research informed by critical theories recognizes that identities are not only multiple and dynamic but also negotiated within different contexts of power. When individuals draw on language to perform identities, language not only constructs meaning but also imposes power. Highlighting this dynamic, Gumperz (1982) notes that

> Language differences play an important, positive role in signalling information as well as in creating and maintaining the subtle boundaries of power, status, role and occupational specialisation that make up the fabric of our social life. Assumptions about value differences associated with these boundaries in fact form the very basis for the indirect communicative strategies employed in key gatekeeping encounters. (pp. 6–7)

From this perspective, every encounter involving intercultural communication is a site of struggle where meanings are negotiated and strategies are employed to assert the legitimacy of one's statements. To participate in such encounters, speakers need to negotiate structures and relations of power that can position them in unequal ways. Davies and Harré (1990) use the term "position" as "the central organising concept for analysing how it is that people do being a person" (p. 62). They and other poststructuralist theorists have asserted that identities are contingent, shifting, and context dependent, and that while identities or positions are often given by social structures or ascribed by others, subject positions can also be negotiated by agents who wish to position themselves in more powerful ways. As Davies and Harré note, "discursive practices constitute the speakers and hearers in certain ways and yet at the same time are a resource through which speakers and hearers can negotiate new positions" (1990, p. 62). Identity, practices, and resources are mutually constitutive, and while some inscriptions of identity (e.g., race, gender, and ethnicity) may limit and constrain opportunities to speak, certain subject positions may offer enhanced sets of possibilities for social interaction and human agency, that is, the possibility to take action in social settings. Operating within the tensions of structure and agency, individuals who struggle to speak from one position may be able to reframe their relationship with others and claim more powerful, alternative identities (Norton, 2013).

For Darvin and Norton (2015), this critical perspective of identity intersects with notions of ideology and capital, which together shape the way individuals invest in specific discursive practices. Originally conceptualized by Norton (2000) to capture the historical and material relationship of learners with a target language, investment is a construct that draws attention to how speakers negotiate relations of power in ways that shape how they participate in different communicative contexts. When speakers interact with others in intercultural contexts, for instance, they may *invest* in the discursive practices of this context to varying degrees. If they are recognized as legitimate participants, as individuals who hold a rightful place in such a context, they can be fully invested in the exchange, but if they are positioned as unworthy or as Other, they may choose to withdraw or disinvest from this encounter. To dissect the power dynamics of such an interaction, Darvin and Norton (2015) draw on Bourdieu's (1990) concept of habitus to understand how people position themselves and others, granting or refusing them power. For Bourdieu (1990), habitus is "a system of durable, transposable dispositions ... principles which generate and organize practices and representations" (p. 53). Aligned with Holland and Lave's (2001) notion of "history in person," habitus is durable because it is constructed across time and reproduced through different social practices. As a set of dispositions, habitus provides a conceptual understanding of what is reasonable and possible to think and act in specific ways. It configures in individuals an idea of their rightful place in society and predisposes them to do what they believe is expected of them and to develop relations that are deemed appropriate.

This habitus or disposition, this sense of place in the social world, involves an internalization of ideologies, "dominant ways of thinking that organize and stabilize societies while simultaneously determining modes of inclusion and exclusion" (Darvin & Norton, 2015, p. 44). Through naturalized activities and practices, ideology becomes common sense, a way to perceive the world that reproduces existing social relations and power structures (Blommaert, 2005). Ideology is experienced and manufactured through discourse, and it is through "ideological imaginations of culture" (Holliday, 2010, p. 2) that foreign Others can be essentialized and demonized. Promulgated within institutional frames, the power of ideology is its ability to render itself invisible, making it difficult to resist or contest. Neoliberal ideology, for instance, with its logic of profit and market forces, is able to embed itself not just in systems of governance, but also in ways of thinking about the value of languages (Duchêne & Heller, 2012) and their speakers (Tupas, 2015). Holliday (2006) describes native-speakerism as a pervasive ideology that accords native speakers of a language like English a privileged position in certain intercultural contexts while othering non-native speakers and positioning them as less capable. The linguistic, semiotic, material, and social resources that speakers bring to these contexts constitute their capital, the value of which is shaped by ideology. Capital is power, and speakers can be positioned by the volume, composition, and trajectory of their capital.

In a study of the language and literacy practices of two youth who immigrated to Vancouver from the Philippines, Darvin (2017) demonstrates how social class differences, the unequal access to material and symbolic resources, shaped these young people's dispositions toward language and the way they position themselves as immigrants. The son of a wealthy entrepreneur, Ayrton immigrated to Canada with his family through the Investor category and lives in a wealthy part of Vancouver. He believes that "with how the world is just connected and how information is at your fingertips, you can be anyone or anything you want to be and it's just right there" (p. 302). This powerful sense of agency is matched by his confidence in speaking English, which he spoke growing up in Manila. Referring to his use of English in Vancouver, he says, "I feel that I didn't need to adjust my English ... I'm just slowly being influenced in speaking English" (p. 303). He expresses ownership of the language ("my English") and asserts his legitimate place as a resident of Canada. Referring to his classmates in the private school he goes to, most of whom come from wealthy families, he shares, "The moment I tell them I'm Filipino they wouldn't believe me mainly because I don't look like someone who's from the Philippines" (p. 303). He mentions that the only other Filipinos in his school are those who work at the cafeteria or as part of maintenance. Ayrton seems to take pride in not being recognized as Filipino, and in this case ethnicity intersects with class, the subtext being that in this private high school that caters for the upper class, he is not positioned as someone from a Global South country like the Philippines.

Like Ayrton, John is also sixteen, but goes to a public school in the east side of Vancouver. He moved to Canada when he was ten, after six years of being separated from his mother who started working in the country as a caregiver under temporary migrant worker conditions. He lives in a one-bedroom apartment with his mother and two siblings, and they speak primarily Filipino at home, which was also the case when they lived in a rural area of the Philippines. Asked what it was like moving to Canada, John says he felt "like a stranger" and that "I had some accents . . . So it was like hard adjusting my English" (Darvin, 2017, p. 303). Because of the less privileged conditions of his migration, he feels like a "stranger" in this country of settlement and thus needs to actively "adjust" the way he speaks to conform to what he regards as native speaker standards and to overcome the accent which is a mark of his own Filipino identity. "Since English is the main language of the world so you can talk to more people. But in Philippines, you can only talk to like only that zone . . . Therefore like if you're in trouble I guess you can be able to communicate with them . . . You could ask them for help" (p. 304).

In this quote, John views his speaking Filipino as a limitation, in that it only allows him to talk to a "zone," a specific group of people, and thus it has no global market value, indexing specific ideologies about what makes languages "valuable." He believes that English is "the main language of the world" and even though he speaks English himself, he still views English speakers as other, as "them," and relegates himself to a position of powerlessness and vulnerability. He has to learn to "communicate with them" so that he can "ask them for help," attributing power to those who speak what he believes is standard English. By articulating this belief, John demonstrates how he has internalized ideologies that privilege so-called native speakers of English, and consequently, wealthy nation-states like Canada from where these native speakers originate. Such ideological assumptions are deeply entrenched in the collective unconscious of a nation like the Philippines that has been colonized by the United States, and where English as a colonizing tool has been effective in segregating society into those who have the capital to achieve fluency in a colonial language and those who do not. In this labor brokerage state, discourses of progress reproduce ideologies of migration and language: that migration benefits only the migrant, not the receiving nation, and that one must achieve native speaker standards to assert a legitimate place in intercultural contexts.

3 Performing Identity

Recognizing that identity is discursively produced and without an essential core, Butler (1990) asserts that it is performed in ways that are transient and iterative, and where identity is "performatively constituted by the very 'expressions' that are said to be its results" (p. 33). Subjects can exercise agency through the integration of new elements and disruptive tropes, but identity is always produced through discourse. Performed vis-à-vis diverse relations and contexts, identity is fluid, as it is constructed, mediated, and negotiated in different ways. While the meanings of these terms overlap, this section discusses how each term provides a nuanced way of examining how identities are performed.

3.1 Identity as Constructed

Aligned with the poststructuralist notion that subjectivities are continually constructed through language (Hall, 1996, 2012), Blommaert (2005) describes identity as "particular forms of semiotic potential, organised in a repertoire" (p. 207). Rather than being a property or stable category of individuals, it is constructed by configuring or assembling semiotic resources through practices or socially conditioned semiotic work. Hence, identity is always performed or enacted, and also has to be recognized by others or members of a community that one aligns with. As linguistic and semiotic resources are used to perform identities, individuals can adopt linguistic styles or expressions that may index geographical origin, gender, age, or class, and demonstrate membership in specific social groupings or identity categories. This *indexicality* signals how acts of communication produce (or index) social meanings. The word "sir," for instance, does not only refer to a male individual, but also indexes a specific social status. Every utterance indexes something about the identity of the person who utters it and the social context in which it is uttered (Blommaert, 2005). This constructionist view of identity extends to understandings of culture. Instead of viewing culture as something people belong to, it can be examined as a process: something people do or perform (Piller, 2017). As an abstract and analytical notion, culture "does not cause behaviour, but summarises an abstraction from it, and is thus neither normative nor predictive" (Baumann, 1996, p. 11). In the same vein, the constructed nature of identity highlights how it is emergent, dynamic, continually shifting. Researchers engage in detailed analysis of language in interactions and discursive practices to understand the extent to which interlocutors invoke, align with, or resist cultural memberships (Zhu, 2014).

In a sociolinguistic ethnographic study examining the cultural and linguistic practices of people in four UK cities, Zhu and Li (2020) closely observed the life of M, an artist of Polish origin living in London. The researchers were particularly interested in how multilingual speakers drew on their linguistic resources to construct multiple identities and to negotiate "misalignment between identities she aligns to and identities assigned by others" (p. 240). M, for instance, resisted being typecast as a Polish migrant on stage, and was reluctant to use

Polish when her collaborators suggested she use this linguistic resource when the character she was playing gets angry in one scene. When the researchers interviewed her regarding this conversation with the collaborators, she said (the length of pause in seconds in indicated in brackets):

> I have to have a good reason and I didn't think that at that point in our piece the reason was strong enough if my character or anybody else's character had a reason to speak a different language sure but [3] I didn't want to make it about Polish language just [2] for the sake of it I didn't want it to be I didn't want to at any point have a conversation about migration or be the token foreigner. (M, interview in Zhu & Li, 2020, p. 241)

In another situation, M was discussing with a fellow actor the possibility of his character using English words in the play that M would genuinely not understand, so that during the performance, she could truthfully say she did not understand what he said. At one point of this discussion, M uttered "me no English Polish migrant" with a stylized foreign accent, before saying in her usual voice, "I don't want to play that." M used the utterance "me no English Polish migrant" to index a specific stereotype, but with the purpose of drawing attention to such a stereotype in order to subvert it. Zhu and Li (2020) point out how M mobilized her semiotic resources, engaging in language play and double voicing to actively construct different identities and to employ a subversive yet playful approach to resist an essentialized identity ascribed by others.

3.2 Identity as Fluid

To say that identity is fluid is to recognize that it is not fixed or stable, but rather it can shift from moment to moment, and change across time and space. When migrants cross borders through varying immigration categories for instance – as investors, professionals, refugees, or students – they perform multiple identities. Driven by diverse goals, serving different needs of nation-states, and equipped with varying levels of economic, cultural, and social capital, immigrants, sojourners, and migrant workers occupy different social locations in their adopted or host country. With the rapid advancement of technology, the structures of migrant socialization have changed, as have patterns of migrant movement and employment. Through more affordable travel costs, mobile communication devices, social media, and online connectivity, migrant learners are increasingly able to navigate more seamlessly between their countries of origin and of settlement, and pursue their lives with a greater sense of transnationalism (Basch et al., 1994). Because these boundaries have been eroded, the arenas in which migrants participate and exchange economic, social, and cultural capital have become much wider and more complex. They can no longer be understood just as migrants on a local or national scale. Traversing deterritorialized spaces, where culture transcends geographical demarcations (Appadurai, 1990), they operate as transnationals who are able to maintain ties with their home country while building new relations within their host or adopted country.

Recognizing how the processes of globalization have made us rethink ideas of homogeneity and nation-states, Pennycook (2007) uses the term *transcultural flows* to foreground "the ways in which cultural forms move, change and are reused to fashion new identities in diverse contexts" (p. 6), enabling processes of borrowing, blending, and remaking. Risager (2006) points out how these flows shape "unconscious patterns of behaviour that are not so easy to change and which are linked to the identity of the individual" (p. 180). Given these eroding boundaries of culture and language, Canagarajah (2013) has made the case for translingual practice that foregrounds how language resources are mobile, fluid, and hybrid. Recognizing that languages are inventions (Makoni & Pennycook, 2007) and ideological constructions that arose alongside the emergence of the nation-state (Blommaert & Rampton, 2011), translanguaging signals the notion that communication transpires through the deployment of diverse linguistic features that may be identified with but are not necessarily bound to certain social and cultural associations. While this translingual orientation involves not according labeled languages and varieties with an ontological status, they acquire "labels and identities through situated uses in particular contexts" (Canagarajah, 2013, p. 15). As people move across borders, the linguistic resources they bring with them are subject to different orders of indexicality, that is, their styles and registers are measured against a value system that reflects the biases and assumptions of the larger sociocultural context (Blommaert, 2007). Functions that are valid in local settings are imposed on the ways of speaking of transnationals, and discourses only gain value when others grant them, based on their market value. The English of urban Africans within local African contexts may carry prestige and afford middle-class identities, but when spoken in London it becomes a stigmatizing resource that positions them as lower class (Blommaert, 2005).

In a study of two transnational Mexican youth in the United States, Lam and Christiansen (2022) draw on the concept of Bakhtin's (1981) chronotopes or time–space frames to understand how youth constructed their identities and cultivated relationships with communities in Mexico. Born in the United States with parents from Guanajuato in Mexico, fifteen-year-old Alexandra spends a lot of time with her cousins during visits to her parents' hometown. She stays up to date on their lives via Facebook, and enjoys watching Spanish-language videos from Mexico, other parts of Latin America, and Spain. While showing the researcher old photos on Facebook, she pointed out members of her family at her uncle's wedding.

*Luego Micaela, Daniel, Omar, así como lo ve de chiquito, ya está bien alto. Y mi primo Marcos, Agapito, este también estaba bien chiquito y ya está bien grande. Ahorita se lo enseño. Y ésta es Rosa. Es Fernanda. Es la que **se nos** va a casar.*

[And then there's Micaela, Daniel, Omar, he's very small here, but he's very tall now. And my cousin Marcos, Agapito, he was also small but now he's very tall. I'll show you right now. And this is Rosa. This is Fernanda. She's the one who is going to get married **on us**.] (Alexandra, interview, in Lam & Christiansen, 2022, p. 12)

When Alexandra refers to Fernanda while talking about the upcoming wedding, she uses the reflexive third person pronoun (*se nos*/on us) to include herself in the immediate family and to suggest direct involvement with the bride. This linguistic choice asserts her affiliation with her cousins in Mexico and makes herself relevant to a wedding she would likely not attend. Through social media, she departs from her "local identities to create a different version of [herself] not tied to a particular location nor bound by time" (Lam & Christiansen, 2022, p. 15). Referring to her experiences speaking Spanish in Mexico, she says:

Te dicen, "Ah, ustedes son de afuera." Que no sé qué. "No, somos de aquí." Nomás que no sé porqué dicen que tengo un acento raro. Y ya en la semana estamos hablando como ellos. Y se nos pega.

[They tell you, "Ah, you guys must be foreigners." Or I don't know what. We'll say, "No, we're from here." I just don't know why they say I have a strange accent. And in a week we're talking like them. And it sticks.] (In Lam & Christiansen, 2022, p. 16)

Even though she recognized that they spoke their own variety of Spanish, Alexandra does not understand why she is identified as a foreigner and resists being treated as Other ("No, we're from here."). She perceives accent "as a marker of her fluid movement across locales" (Lam & Christiansen, 2022, p. 16), particularly as she adopts multiple varieties of Spanish in her linguistic repertoire.

3.3 Identity as Negotiated

Apart from being constructed and fluid, we say that identity is *negotiated* to signal how it is shaped through interaction and involves navigating existing social practices, structures, and institutions. During intercultural encounters, speakers negotiate their material and symbolic resources to position themselves in specific ways. Access to these identity-building resources is unequal, and so is how these resources are valued in different ideological spaces, and thus the process of negotiation also indexes asymmetrical relations of power. By understanding the sociopolitical contexts and structural forces speakers contend with in such encounters, we can better understand how they appropriate language to claim power (De Costa, 2010). When speakers negotiate their identities in specific contexts, they can be positioned by others in terms of their race, gender, ethnicity, class, sexual orientation, and so on. Intersectionality recognizes that while people can be positioned because of a specific inscription of their identity (e.g., being "Black," "a woman," or "gay"), these dimensions actually interrelate or intersect. The lived experiences of a working-class Black lesbian will be markedly different from those of a middle-class white heterosexual man, and identity researchers need to recognize that there are variations and inequalities within these dimensions (Block & Corona, 2014). The situation of struggling immigrant students cannot be attributed solely to inscriptions of race or ethnicity but must be examined with respect to other categories such as class and gender.

In a study that examines the intersection of race, gender, and sexuality, Appleby (2013) provides insight into the experiences of heterosexual white Australian men while teaching in commercial conversation schools in Japan that cater to a largely female clientele. While the men enjoyed the privileges attached to being a white, Western male, they also had to negotiate their professional identity in this eikaiwa industry where the extroverted and eroticized white male teacher was produced as a commodity for Japanese customer-students. In this intercultural domain where the educational converged with the commercial, policies on teacher–student fraternization were ambiguous, and men were encouraged to perform an ideal of Western masculinity. During the interviews, participants would describe themselves in relation to the cultural trope of the Charisma Man, an "average guy" from the West that becomes a "superhero" in Japan, and that Appleby (2013) describes as "an ironic self-positioning of contemporary Western masculinity which is dependent on, and accountable to, the female gaze" (p. 129). Expected to embody a romanticized version of the West, the men had to negotiate their identities as white, heterosexual male teachers in relation to not only their employers, their female students, and fellow teachers, but also the researcher. Appleby (2013) notes how she became increasingly aware of how the men would intentionally distance themselves from the obnoxious characteristics of the Charisma Man "to construct—through the articulation of perceptions and experiences—a version of themselves and their masculinity, that society (and [the researcher]) might consider acceptable" (p. 133). This reflexive observation foregrounds how identities are always negotiated in social interaction, in response to different contexts and interlocutors.

3.4 Identity as Mediated

Mediation involves the use of tools to perform certain actions, and these tools can be physical objects or abstract codes like language. By mediating actions, tools become extensions of ourselves and transform what we can do and mean, how we think and relate to others, and who we can be (Jones & Hafner, 2021). In the digital world, identity is mediated by continually evolving technologies like phones, apps, and social media platforms, where we can document and display our lives through various modalities.

This presentational culture, where multiple aspects of one's life are shared with different kinds of audiences, alters notions of private and public spaces and affects the way we perceive ourselves (Barton & Lee, 2013). By connecting us with diverse others and enabling new language practices, online spaces have become increasingly important intercultural arenas for the development of identities. Within these networked publics (boyd, 2014), speakers negotiate shared values and norms of collective behavior while differentiating themselves in online interactions and participating in a range of online discourse communities. Whether we are emailing a colleague, tweeting to the general public, or posting a status update on Facebook, we adapt digital affordances to specific contexts, relations, and identities.

Stornaiuolo and colleagues (2009) argue that such limitless options complexify, extend, and change self-identifications. By communicating across multiple symbolic systems in the online world, individuals can imagine new identities and ways of being in the world. They are able to share these self-representations with diverse audiences, who may interpret the meanings of these representations in very different ways. When users perform identities in different apps, these social media platforms do not just mediate interaction; they constitute it (Gillespie, 2018). Van Dijck et al. (2018) contend that a platform operates with a specific logic, the set of principles that guide how information is processed and social traffic is channeled. This programmability enables platforms to "trigger and steer users' creative or communicative contributions" (p. 5). As users interact with others online, the design and infrastructure of online spaces have the power to construct conditions of possibility for sociality in these spaces (Bucher, 2018). They assemble what linguistic and semiotic resources they have at their disposal, and the architecture of the platform also defines the parameters of what they are able to deploy.

As users negotiate their own intentions with the affordances and constraints of a platform and the contextual aspects of different communicative events, certain patterns or practices surrounding platform use emerge. These cultures-of-use (Thorne, 2016) are "historically sedimented associations, purposes, and values" (p. 185) that accrue to a platform and generate expectations of genre-specific activity.

Such interactional and relational associations together with expectations of genre-specific activity are learned through processes of platform socialization. As users of a platform negotiate cultures-of-use and designs that program interactions in certain ways, they can be steered toward certain behaviors that may afford or constrain possibilities for identity work. It is by adeptly navigating the social and material landscapes of these platforms that users are able to find opportunities for expression and connection that assert their own identities and membership in specific communities.

In a study of the language practices of Filipino domestic workers in Hong Kong, Darvin (2022a) presents Karina, whose curation of her posts on Facebook and TikTok enables her to perform different identities for diverse audiences, and such differences shape the way she assembles her linguistic and semiotic resources online. In her Facebook profile, she uses her real name and showcases her identity as a mother, with pictures of her three children as her cover photo. To avoid speculation from family and friends in the Philippines, she identifies as "Single" even though she has a boyfriend in Hong Kong. By requiring users to input specific information in given fields, the design or architecture of a Facebook profile structures not only the semiotic resources Karina chooses, but also arranges which aspects of her identity can be foregrounded (i.e., education, place of residence, hometown, relationship status, etc.). In contrast, the design of a TikTok profile enables Karina to choose a pseudonym, and to create her own description in a bio field with a maximum of eighty characters without having to enter her location. Given these affordances, Karina is able to perform a TikTok identity different from the mother she presents herself as on Facebook. Her username is @karinalicious01 (revised to maintain privacy but structured similarly to reflect the original, i.e., @[real name]licious01). In this account she has almost 10,000 followers, mostly from Hong Kong, and she posts videos of herself dancing or lipsyncing in skimpy outfits. One of the hashtags that Karina often uses in her TikTok posts is #hkpagal_____ (the English suffix that follows is stricken out to maintain anonymity). According to Karina, "pagal" is "crazy" in Urdu and the reason she has such a hashtag is that her group of female Filipino friends is connected with a group of male Pakistani friends, and they have appeared on each other's TikToks and use the hashtag to connect with each other on the platform. This form of social tagging (Lee, 2018) has become one of the reasons that Karina meets more Pakistanis on TikTok since those who follow a fellow member and click on the hashtag can then be led to other members' videos. By providing different affordances and constraints, social media platforms mediate identity and intercultural encounters online. As an assemblage of sociotechnical structures (Darvin, 2023), platform design shapes various cultures-of-use, encouraging specific ways of representing oneself, and enabling interactions with diverse others.

4 Categorizing Identity

Given how culture is fluid, complex, and emergent, the notion of a "cultural identity" has been debated in language and intercultural communication research (e.g., Holliday, 2013; Kramsch, 2009; Piller, 2017). In its nominal form, the term can be viewed as static, fixed, and ambiguous in terms of which "culture" this identity should refer to, particularly when such a term involves intersecting categories of race, ethnicity, nationality, class, and others. While these categories themselves are socially constructed and fluid, they are particularly useful in dissecting how culture becomes relevant in particular intercultural situations, that is, how people position themselves through a process of identification and how they are positioned by others through a process of ascription. People may identify as Black, Chinese, Filipino, or middle class in specific situations where they find such categories meaningful. At the same time, people can ascribe these identities to others, particularly as they are made visible on their bodies, their accents, or the documents they carry. These inscriptions of identity (Block, 2012) are audible and visible cues that are "inscribed" or attached to bodies: the way we look, speak, and dress. These cues render us legible to others, and it is during intercultural situations that such differences can be interpreted as "cultural differences" and that the intercultural line is drawn to separate the Self and the Other (Holliday, 2010). While race and ethnicity are themselves constructed in interaction, and ethnicity can incorporate nation-state affiliations (e.g., Indian, Pakistani, Filipino, etc.), these identity categories are made salient because interlocutors regard them as relevant.

Drawing attention to how these inscriptions of identity are implicated in relations of power, Pavlenko and Blackledge (2004) propose three types of identities: "*imposed identities* (which are not negotiable in a particular time and place), *assumed identities* (which are accepted and not negotiated), and *negotiable identities* (which are contested by groups and individuals)" (p. 21). Assumed identities are those valued and legitimated by dominant ideologies (e.g., heterosexual, middle class, male, etc.), while imposed identities are ascribed by those in power (e.g., governments, immigration officers, etc.) to people who cannot resist such assignations, and negotiable identities are those that particular individuals and groups can contest and resist. At the same time, people can self-identify with specific categories, and at times even adopt what Spivak (1996) calls a strategic essentialism in which people mobilize on the basis of a shared racial, ethnic, national, or class identity.

4.1 Race and Ethnicity

Race and ethnicity have long been researched as inscriptions of identity, and for Zhu (2014), "ethnicity and race are central to cultural identity to the extent that ethnic or racial identities are often conflated with cultural identity in practice" (p. 204). Recognizing how these two categories often overlap, Block (2022) points out how in the 2020 census of the United States, there are markers of geographical location (nation-state names) and ethnicity ("African American," "Hispanic," "Latino") alongside race ("Black," "white"). While historically race has been used to refer to "a biological classification system determined by physical characteristics of genetic origin" (Sue, 2003, p. 34), race is an ideological construct where the boundaries between groups have been historically and socially produced (MacMaster, 2001). This constructedness applies as well to ethnicity, which can be understood as "a form of collective identity based on shared cultural beliefs and practices, such as language, history, descent, and religion" (Puri, 2004, p. 174). Highlighting this link to language, Blommaert (2005) uses the term *ethnolinguistic identity* to refer to "an identity expressed through belonging to a particular language community and articulated in settlements such as 'I speak Dutch', 'I am British [*ergo* I speak English]'" (p. 214).

For De Fina (2007), ethnicity can only be understood as it is constructed and negotiated in concrete social practices. In an ethnographic study of an all-male card-playing club in Washington, DC called Circolo that brings together Italian-born and US-born adults, the researcher demonstrates how Italian ethnic identity is a core feature of the organization. Through public addresses, storytelling, and forms of socialization, Circolo is constructed as essentially Italian with many of its activities as shaped by Italian traditions. One such socialization practice is welcoming new members to the club and teaching them card games like *Briscola* or *Tressette*, including basic words of the game in Italian. In this excerpt, the President and Rob are teaching Andy, who has just recently joined the club. All the players are American born, and only the President is fluent in Italian.[1]

> 01 Pres.: You know the basic rules of playing?
> 02 Rob: Do you want to play an open hand?
> 03 Pres.: Do you think you need to play an open hand?
> 04 Andy: Ya.

---

[1] In this transcription, @ refers to laughter.

05 Pres.: Okay.

06 Andy: I do, //that's what everybody else does.

07 Rob: //That's what I normally do with people who don't know how to play.

08 Pres.: Do an open hand, *una mano aperta*.

09 Andy: Is that// okay?

10 Pres.: //Do you speak any Italian?

11 Andy: Spanish.

12 Pres.: Just Spanish?

13 Andy: @@@

14 Pres.: No Italian?

15 Andy: I'll use my grandmother and him ((addressing his grandfather)) to talk, that's it.

16 Rob: At least they don't fight, that's good.

17 Andy: They're always fighting when they talk, all the time.

18 Pres.: ((To all)) Andy doesn't say a word of Italian. How did that happen? @@ (from De Fina, 2007, p. 385)

Through code-switching, the situational identity of card player is connected with a collective Italian identity, and the inability to speak any Italian positions one as an outsider. Rather than being a fixed property, Italian ethnicity is relationally produced and emerges as a common frame of reference for people with different social backgrounds, origins, and language competence (De Fina, 2007).

This mapping of language to ethnicity and race, however, can also be challenged by the way speakers adopt styles that do not necessarily correspond with their ethnic or racial identity. In a landmark study of ethnicity and youth in late industrial Britain, Rampton (2017) draws on ethnographic research to examine "language crossing" where friends of Anglo and Afro-Caribbean descent would use Punjabi, or where Anglos and Punjabis would use Creole, and when all of them would use stylized Indian English. Through this language sharing and exchange, they negotiated their ethnic identities and participated in "the enunciation of interethnic youth, class and neighbourhood community" (p. 19). In another study of two Laotian American teenage girls from a diverse high school in California, Bucholtz (2004) demonstrates how these youth use their linguistic resources to perform either of two stereotypes: the model-minority nerd or the dangerous gangster. By using African American vernacular English and youth slang, they produced a linguistic style that positioned them outside of the school's Black/white racial ideology.

A number of scholars have also examined the relationship between race and language learning (Curtis & Romney, 2006; Flores & Rosa, 2015; Kubota

& Lin, 2009; Lin et al., 2004; McKinney, 2007; Motha, 2006). In a study of African American study abroad college participants who learned Portuguese in Brazil, Anya (2011, 2017) found that these Black students were drawn by the desire to connect with and learn more about Afro-descendant speakers of their target language, while Feinauer and Whiting (2012), who studied Latinx communities in the United States, demonstrated how an emerging ethnic identity among preadolescent language minority youth needed to be supported in schools to protect them from discrimination and othering. During intercultural encounters, learners can be positioned based on their ascribed ethnic or racial identities. In a study of immigrant learners, for instance, Gunderson (2007) notes how Mandarin and Cantonese speakers were considered to be from affluent families while Vietnamese speakers were understood to be refugees with limited economic capital. The racialization and marginalization of specific ethnic groups can thus be read as corollary to subordination within neocolonialism and global capitalism, and the very act of migration sometimes becomes understood as the natural result of the underdevelopment of specific countries.

4.2 Nationality

Nationality refers to an individual's perception of belonging to a nation-state. For Anderson (1991) nations are imagined communities, "because the members of even the smallest nation will never know most of their fellow-members, meet them, or even hear of them, yet in the minds of each lives the image of their communion" (p. 6).While the notions of nation and nationality are imagined and constructed through discourse, Holliday (2013) recognizes the role of nations in cultural identification, providing an external cultural reality that enables a framing of identities (Baker, 2015). Through the discourses of banal nationalism constructed and reproduced by governments, schools, media, and state institutions, people can be socialized into particular subject positions, regard themselves as members of a particular nation, and be predisposed to specific activities. At the same time, people can resist these nationalist discourses by attaching to more local identities. In Hong Kong, for instance, when its relatively autonomous status as a special administrative region (SAR) of China was threatened by establishment of an extradition bill that would have made it possible to extradite Hong Kong residents to mainland China, there was a rise in the number of people in the city who identified as Hongkonger, a resident of Hong Kong. During this period of great political unrest, a survey conducted by the University of Hong Kong showed that the number of people who adopted this local Hongkonger identity rose to 76 percent, the highest since the handover of the city to China in 1997. At the same time, those who identified as "Chinese" which signified a national identity was at a record low of 23 percent (HKUPOP, 2019). In earlier surveys, these contrasting identifications have been linked to categories of social class, educational attainment, and age (Steinhardt et al., 2018) as younger members of the population, those with greater material security and higher education were more likely to adopt a Hongkonger identity.

While self-identifications of nationality can shift in different sociopolitical contexts, people can also position others in ways that conflate language, race, and nationality. In a study of white undergraduates who speak English as a first language at a southwestern US university, Shuck (2006) found that non-native speakers with non-European origins were seen by the students as incomprehensible, intellectually lesser, and responsible for their "non-integration" into American society. Students born in the United States can view whiteness and nativeness in English as unmarked and subscribe to the notion that foreigners have accents while Americans do not; the onus is always on the non-native speaker, not the white student, to create comprehensibility. In the following situation, Jen complains about two teaching assistants (TAs) by constructing racial categories and making links to national origin.

Jen: I took—..what did I take. . . . MATH..121 last semester. . . . and . . . my
TA:, . . . was <[high pitch] very ni:ce, [high pitch]> ..but she was
fro:m—..I don't know where she was from. . .an Asian-speaking country
though. . . . because she was Asian.
. . . I had no clue, ..what she said, ..the whole semester, [. . .]..I ended up
talking to the professor, . . . and it was like..this WEIRD English class,
where..it was experimental— I mean, ..math class, sorry, . . . and..they
had five—it was a five-hundred person lecture, . . . had I known this, I
wouldn't have taken it, /but/ I didn't know.
G: /hm./
Jen: ..a:nd, ..then they had TAs there. . .and during the lecture, you'd ask the
TA if you had a question or whatever. . . . couldn't..understand..what
she said. and..I didn't want to like..hurt her feelings or whatever,
G: Mhm. Mhm.=
Jen: [. . .] . . . so, ..I started checking in with her,
 and going, [taps table]
..to sit, [taps table]
..by this OTHER guy. [taps table]
. . . who I assumed . . . spoke . . . um— . . . or, wh- I s- I assumed he was
from America. . .okay? 'cause he was like Caucasian, . . . he (wa?)s
from New Zealand.
G: hm.
Jen: . . . couldn't understand . . . what..HE said.

(from Shuck, 2006, p. 265)

Jen positions both her teachers as foreign and incomprehensible, referring to their races ("Asian," "Caucasian") and nationality ("from New Zealand"). Ideological models reproduce a hierarchical social order where US-born citizens, native English speakers, and whiteness retain a privilege that is linked to American-ness. As transnationalism opens up multiple spaces, Kelly (2012) points out that the racialized identities of migrants can still often be based upon their country of origin, and being from a specific country begins to imply a certain aptitude or suitability for specific occupations. Countries of origin, themselves implicated in a global class hierarchy, can position migrants in ways that refract this world economic order. The transnational affiliations of speakers may vary depending on the distance between host and home countries, the economic relations between them, cross-border policies, the legal status and context of migrants, and the politics and media capabilities of both countries of origin and settlement (Lam & Warriner, 2012).

4.3 Class

While class has always been recognized as an economic position, it has also increasingly been regarded as a cultural process, marked by consumption patterns, identity formations, and bodily attributes like accent, behavior, and dress (Kelly, 2012). The volume and composition of one's capital, whether economic, cultural, or social, constitutes one's location in a class hierarchy, and in intercultural encounters, speakers can be positioned based on such class differences. In a study of the lived experiences of Spanish-speaking migrants in London, Block (2012) demonstrates how one migrant's class position, indexed by his educational attainment, consumption patterns, and symbolic behavior, shaped feelings of ambivalence in different intercultural spaces. Carlos is a 42-year-old Colombian man with a PhD in philosophy from a Colombian university. Because of his relatively poor English language competence, he had to take a job as a porter, but while he did not have a large salary, he and his wife owned two properties in Greater London, which they rented out. Referring to a conversation about football that he had with a coworker, Dan, who has a marked working-class and Cockney accent, Carlos says:

> *es duro entender a Dan / porque si escuchaste la grabación (.5) creo que para*
> *los mismos ingleses / es muy cerrado su inglés / el corta mucho las frases / las*
> *palabras las reduce / las comprime mucho / entonces llega un momento en*
> *que es agotador seguirle la conversación / y ya bueno / lo haces simplemente*
> *por escucharlo / y de pronto te hace una pregunta / y tu la coges por ahí y (1)*
> *pero después de un momento / después de unos diez minutos / ya la*
> *conversación fluye / pero de lado de el / sin haber ninguna significación*
> *<laughing> / porque es muy muy . . .*

it's hard to understand Dan / because if you listened to the recording (.5) I think that even for English people / his English is very closed / he cuts his sentences a lot / he reduces words / he compresses them a lot / so it gets to a point when it's exhausting to follow his conversation / and well / you're just there to listen to him / and then suddenly he asks you a question / and you do the best you can and (1) but after a while / after about ten minutes / the conversation flows / but from his side / without any meaning <laughing> / because he's very very . . . (Interview with Carlos, from Block, 2012, p. 198)

During this workplace conversation he refers to, where the phatic is more important than the transactional, Carlos explains how the biggest issue he finds is Dan's pronunciation ("his English is very closed" and "he cuts his sentences a lot"). While he does not understand some turns of phrase by Dan, Carlos has adapted this class positioning not merely as a passive listener but as one who can engage in repartee and talk about English football, which can be regarded as a working-class topic. Outside of work, Carlos' lifestyle remains very much middle class in terms of his consumption patterns and symbolic behavior. He maintains an interest in international cinema and literature and makes short weekend trips to European cities, and this class positioning despite his limited English provides him with confidence in other intercultural encounters.

la experiencia mia anterior / digamos académica (.5) te da confianza para ir al médico / por ejemplo / para hacer un poco las cosas en tu vida normal / pero es un poco sentirse como afianzado en esa situación intelectual que te permite como ganar la confianza / y he pensado también / o he visto que la gente que no tiene / digamos / ese sustento (.5) es más débil / es más venerable . . .

my previous experience / let's say academic (.5) gives you confidence to go to the doctor / for example / to kind of do things in your normal life / but it's a little like feeling strengthened by that intellectual situation that allows you to gain confidence / And I have thought about this as well / or I have seen how the people who don't have / let's say / this support (.5) are weaker / more vulnerable . . . (Interview with Carlos, from Block, 2012, p. 200)

By recognizing how Carlos' intercultural experiences are marked by class, the study demonstrates how class intersects with other inscriptions of identity such as race, ethnicity, and nationality. Block (2012) notes that while Carlos was positioned by fellow workers in terms of his middle-class behavior and educational background, that he was Colombian and of mixed African and Amerindian ancestry also figured into his interactions with his white working-class coworkers from London. Whenever workplace conversations would refer to Colombia, he would find how these would involve stereotypical images of drug traffickers, poverty, and violence.

5 Contextualizing Identity

As a construct that involves "how a person understands his or her relationship to the world" (Norton, 2013, p. 45), identity foregrounds how intercultural interactions are always situated and contextualized, as both context dependent and context producing. Contemporary identity research examines how the self is constructed, negotiated, and mediated in various material and symbolic conditions, and in this section, we review relevant studies in the field to demonstrate the intricacies of these processes as they shape intercultural interactions, both online and offline. In selecting studies to review in this section, we focused on studies conducted by applied linguistics researchers with a particular focus on identity work in diverse intercultural contexts. To narrow down these choices further, we referred to the following criteria: first, diverse research populations relevant to intercultural communication (e.g., language learners and teachers, study abroad students, and immigrants from various backgrounds); second, different target/host languages and their varieties (e.g., Cantonese, English, French); third, in addition to including traditionally popular migrant or study abroad destinations (i.e., English-speaking countries and regions), we also included multilingual contexts such as Hong Kong, Japan, and Qatar, where English is not necessarily the first language of the majority of speakers.

In this section, we first focus on language learning/teaching contexts and learn about the experience of a US learner of French (Kinginger, 2004), Japanese learners of English (Miyahara, 2015), and transnational English-speaking teachers in Hong Kong (Gu et al., 2022). We then move on to discuss migration contexts, in particular, the experience of Chinese immigrant families in the UK (Zhu & Li, 2016) and Filipino and Indonesian domestic migrant workers in Hong Kong (Ladegaard, 2019, 2020). Next, we shift our focus to study abroad contexts to look at the experience of a Hong Kong student in New Zealand (Jackson, 2019), US students in France (Whitworth, 2006), and Mainland Chinese STEM students in the United States (Sun, 2020). Then, we consider workplace contexts to understand the communication experience of international teams (Lockwood, 2015), leadership styles in corporation meetings (Chan & Du-Babcock, 2019), migrant workers in New Zealand (Holmes, 2015; Holmes & Riddiford, 2010), American interns in Japan (Moody, 2019), and female academics in Qatar (Al-Khulaifi & Van De Mieroop, 2022). Last but not least, we center on online contexts to examine how language learners (Lam, 2000; Thorne & Black, 2011), language teachers (Dooly, 2011; Ho, 2022), and microcelebrities (Shi et al., 2022) construct and negotiate their fluid, hybrid, and multifaceted identities in digital spaces.

5.1 Language Learning and Teaching

Research in applied linguistics has explored how language learners negotiate their identities in an intercultural context and in the face of marginality and power. Applied linguist Celeste Kinginger (2004) studied the language learning and identity reconstruction of Alice, a US learner of French over a period of four years. The researcher tracked Alice's development from her French learning experiences in the United States to her language immersion in Quebec, and to her international exchange in France. A salient theme that emerged from the participant's narrative was "struggle" (Kinginger, 2004), that is, struggles she experienced throughout her accounts of French learning, resulting from perceived inequitable relations of power. From feeling agonized in front of a more powerful French-speaking partner, to feeling rivalry with a snobbish classmate, and to experiencing ambivalence and frustration with a group of co-nationals in France, Alice's relationship with herself as well as with French learning was constantly in flux. Her access to opportunities was constrained by the more powerful individuals in the context (e.g., a powerful romantic partner, a domineering French teacher, English-speaking co-nationals in her residence hall). This rich, detailed case study reveals how identity can be "a site of struggle" (Norton, 2000, p. 127) over the course of language and (inter)cultural learning. It shows how access (or lack thereof) and power relations can influence the identity negotiation and (re)construction of second/foreign language learners in multiple facets (e.g., linguistic, cultural, personal).

Focusing on Japanese learners of English, Miyahara (2015) explored the L2 identities of Japanese students in an English-medium liberal arts college in Japan. Underpinned by the poststructuralist notion of identity (Norton, 2013) and psychological L2 identity theories (Dörnyei & Ushioda, 2009), the study adopted a narrative-oriented approach to explore the emotive aspects of language learning. It focused on six Japanese students, four of whom ventured abroad for a six-week summer program in an English-speaking country, while two remained nonmobile. Varied types of data (e.g., interview data, journal entries, class discussions, email correspondence) were collected to uncover the participants' identity developmental trajectories. Miyahara (2015) discovered that early positive exposure to English contributed to the case participants' formation of ideal L2 selves (Dörnyei, 2009) as children, whereas a lack of access (e.g., to contextual resources) appeared to hinder the construction of L2 selves (e.g., lack of interactions with first language speakers). For the participants who held a clear, positive vision of an ideal L2 self and of the language, they actively participated in L2 learning and use both in Japan and while abroad. As a result, their L2 identities were "authenticated and strengthened" and their ideal selves "personalise(d)" (p. 103). For those who experienced struggles and frustrations in envisioning their possible L2 selves, the perceived struggle gave them "a degree of agency" (Miyahara, 2015, p. 104). It prompted the learners to recognize linguistic constraints as affordances and to actively act on them, providing opportunities to (re)shape their relationship with the English language and their identities. The author argued that it is not only positive emotions but also negative emotions (e.g., frustration) that can prompt learners to take action for identity development (Miyahara, 2015). The study also provided insight into the role of intercultural communication (e.g., interacting with English-speaking peers and teacher) in contributing to L2 identity development.

Shifting the focus from language learning to language teaching, scholars in the field have also examined the identity (re)construction and negotiation of language teachers (e.g., Barkhuizen, 2017, 2021; Gu, 2018; Gu et al., 2022; Kohler, 2020). Situated in a Hong Kong Chinese context, Gu and colleagues (2022) investigated the identity construction of transnational native-English-speaking teachers (NETs) of Chinese ethnicity who taught in their heritage context. Informed by Foucault's notion of ethical self-formation and research on teacher identity (Clarke, 2019), the study provided a narrative account of two case participants' identity construction in relation to their ethnicity and profession. Michael, who was born and raised in the UK, experienced an "identity crisis" from concealing his bilingual identity when communicating with Cantonese-speaking colleagues. In his narrative, the Chinese aspect in his English–Cantonese bilingual identity "strengthen(ed) his illegitimacy" as a NET teacher in social standards and made him "unreal" (Gu et al., 2022, p. 9). This identity crisis prompted him to question the notion of "NET" in relation to one's ethnic background and linguistic repertoire. Through constructing multiple identities (e.g., a bilingual intercultural communicator, a NET with hidden multilingualism), he was able to renegotiate his space and embrace linguistic/cultural diversity as sources in teaching practice.

Similarly, the other case participant Amelia, with her Chinese appearance and heritage, experienced "illegitimate positioning" (Gu et al., 2022, p. 12) by her Hong Kong local colleagues. In her narrative, local colleagues perceived her "in a strange way" (p. 12) for they failed to acknowledge and respect her unique multilingual identities. To cope, she constructed an alternative NET identity of being proactive, diligent, and willing to cooperate and was able to reclaim her legitimacy and professionalism. The two stories presented by Gu and colleagues (2022) illustrate the complexity of identity negotiation for non-Caucasian NETs in intercultural educational settings. The findings have implications for the intercultural training of language teachers in transnational spaces (e.g., incorporating intercultural knowledge into teaching practice).

5.2 Migrant Families and/or Individuals

Language and intercultural communication researchers have explored the multilingual practice and identity negotiation of immigrants in multilingual and transnational spaces. Research in this area has focused on different groups of people in diverse contexts, for example, Chinese university students and immigrant families in the UK (e.g., Li & Zhu, 2013; Zhu & Li, 2016), Korean immigrant students in Canada (e.g., Kim & Duff, 2012), Korean families in the United States (e.g., Song, 2010), Mexican families in the United States (e.g., Schecter and Bayley, 1997), and Filipino and Indonesian domestic migrant workers in Hong Kong (e.g., Ladegaard, 2019, 2020). These studies have helped us to develop a deeper understanding of the complexity and individuality of transnational experiences in diverse contexts.

Zhu and Li (2016) investigated the impact of transnational experience on and within three Chinese immigrant families from China in the UK, with a focus on family members' identity construction and social relationship building. The researchers adopted a sociolinguistic ethnographic approach and gathered data from fieldwork observation, recordings of family interaction, conversations with family members, and photographs and texts. Data were analyzed using a moment analysis approach (Zhu & Li, 2016), focusing on "spur-of-the-moment" actions that had consequences for the family. The study provided a detailed illustration of the differences in multilingual practices and transnational identity construction of the immigrant families. For the first family under investigation, an indigenous ethnic Korean family from China, maintaining a Korean ethnic identity was prioritized over sustaining Chinese heritage, although they were Chinese passport holders and had never visited Korea before immigrating to the UK. In intercultural interactions, the family preferred to identify themselves as Koreans, not Chinese. This aligned with their multilingual practice of dropping Chinese and maintaining the use of Korean while enhancing their English language skills. The family's social network mainly consisted of Koreans. Their dominant language in social settings was Korean, occasionally mixed with English words. The family's translingual experience revealed their strong ethnic affiliation in their transnational identity negotiation process.

For the British Chinese family in Zhu and Li's (2016) study, they had very different translingual practices. Although the parents had been born and/or raised in the UK to Cantonese-speaking families who originally came from Hong Kong, they put more emphasis on Mandarin than Cantonese in their multilingual practice. The family held a very positive attitude toward Mandarin and was highly invested in Mandarin learning (e.g., watching Chinese TV channels, reading Chinese-language newspapers/magazines regularly). For example, the children dropped out of a Cantonese supplementary school to join a Mandarin supplementary school for "better opportunities in the future." In the mother's account, "Mandarin is the future. China is the future" (Zhu & Li, 2016, p. 661). Also, the family's narrative revealed their transnational affiliation toward China, referring to their short holiday trips to Hong Kong and Mainland China as "return-(ing)" and "go(ing) back" to the homeland (Zhu & Li, 2016, p. 661). Their positive multilingual attitudes facilitated intercultural interaction, as they developed relationships with Mandarin-speaking mainland Chinese in the UK. The family also maintained a wide transnational social network, communicating with friends and relatives in different parts of the world on a weekly basis. They maintained high levels of multilingual and translingual practices.

As for the third immigrant family, the researchers found that the retired Mandarin-speaking couple from China felt lost and isolated in the UK. Their sense of being "at loss" was twofold. First, the couple experienced a disconnection from the Cantonese-speaking Chinese community in the UK, which resulted in a lack of social support network in their daily routine. Second, they experienced a loss of Chinese cultural identity without losing Chinese-language capacity. To be specific, the sense of loss was caused by their inability to comprehend the new Chinese language expressions used by young people, which resulted in their weakened connection with Chinese culture. In their study, Zhu and Li (2016) point out that it is important to recognize the diversity of transnational families and the unique multilingual, transnational experiences of individual families. The researchers call for a holistic and multidimensional perspective for the study of immigrant families' transnational experiences.

Arguing that research in language and intercultural communication has largely focused on elite groups (e.g., international travelers, students, business-people), Ladegaard (e.g., 2017a, 2019, 2020) focused on the experience of a less privileged group, that is, domestic migrant workers. Situated in the context of Hong Kong, his research investigates domestic migrant workers' struggles in identity construction in Hong Kong (e.g., Ladegaard, 2017a), as well as return-ees' remigration back in their home country (e.g., Ladegaard, 2019). Drawing on a corpus of more than 400 narratives of migrant workers in Hong Kong and stories of returnees in the rural Philippines and Indonesia, Ladegaard (2020) reports on the repression, marginalization, and exclusion experienced by migrant workers in Hong Kong. The study used discourse analysis as the analytical method to portray how "self" and "Other" were (re)constructed in identity negotiation.

The narratives of the participants showed that they positioned themselves as "subservient" and were given an ascribed identity by their employers as "stupid," "incompetent," or "useless" based on perceived incompetence in Cantonese, the dominant language in Hong Kong society. Faced with nonrecognition, mistreatment, and verbal and physical abuse, their sense of self was destroyed, and they started to buy into the demeaning discourses constructed by their employers (Ladegaard, 2020, p. 108). Ladegaard points to the language ideologies in Hong Kong, to be specific, of the employers (i.e., incompetence in Cantonese) that were used to flatten and discredit domestic workers' identities. Trying to reclaim legitimacy in their identities, some migrant workers referred to their competence in English to position themselves as more powerful against their Cantonese-speaking employers (e.g., "you better speak in English so that we can understand each other") (Ladegaard, 2020, p. 113). This defensive act created racial distance (we–they discourse) and in-group alignment with other domestic workers who were better educated than their employers. Ladegaard's research highlights the impact of unequal power relations and language ideologies in society on intercultural communication. For underprivileged groups who have an inferior social status, like domestic migrant workers in Hong Kong, "repairing" and regaining a sense of self takes more than just alleged language competence but involves ideological positions in society.

Furthermore, Ladegaard's (2019) investigation of domestic migrant worker returnees in Java, Indonesia illustrates the complex reconceptualization of "self," "home," and "family" for many returnees. Some of the common themes discovered in the returnees' home-coming narratives were reversed cultural shock, alienation from the home culture/community, and pain brought about by the distance and rejection from their own children. Ladegaard (2019) argues that identity negotiation of domestic migrant workers is often dictated by "others," including family members and the patriarchal community that they live in (Ladegaard, 2019). The author calls for more research on less powerful groups in intercultural communication through storytelling (Ladegaard, 2019). With the advancement of technology, digital storytelling (Darvin & Norton, 2014) can create an opportunity for immigrants to make their voices heard in transnational spaces.

5.3 Studying/Traveling Abroad

Identity in intercultural communication has been widely investigated in study abroad contexts, particularly among L2 sojourners (e.g., Benson et al., 2013; Howard, 2019; Humphreys & Baker, 2021; Irie & Ryan, 2015; Jackson, 2018; Ladegaard, 2017b; Mitchell et al., 2017). As Kinginger (2015) observes, student sojourners in an L2 context not only encounter language difficulties but also challenges related to the issue of identity, which to a large extent impact the quality and outcome of study abroad learning. While abroad, sojourners may perform different aspects of identities depending on the context and can experience varying degrees of intercultural engagement and identity expansion.

Student sojourners who venture abroad for an academic semester or year may portray themselves as "ambassadors" of the culture that they come from. For instance, an ethnic Chinese student from a prestigious Hong Kong university, who was enculturated into a Hong Kong Chinese identity, may wish to present themselves as a well-educated, Cantonese-speaking multilingual individual from Asia's world city. This aspect of their avowed identities, however, may not be the same as the identity that is ascribed to them in the host environment. As Jackson (e.g., 2008, 2010) discovered, in some circumstances, Hong Kong students have been ascribed as Mainland Chinese or Japanese nationals while abroad. Critical experiences as such may cause intercultural misunderstanding/conflict, which can have an impact on the sojourners' degree of engagement with the host community. For some sojourners, as the minority in the host environment, a unique Hong Kong Cantonese identity may become more salient and meaningful (e.g., Jackson, 2019) and they may find the changes in their self-identities "threatening" or "disturbing" (Jackson, 2015). Instead of embracing a broadened Chinese/global identity, some participants in Jackson's (2008) study opted to cling to a Hong Kong regional identity and mostly socialized with Hong Kong students while abroad. As a result, they had little exposure to or engagement with the host people/culture and returned home with a more ethnocentric mindset. For others, they may find themselves becoming more attached to their national identity or an "international" self, and less insistent on the recognition of a regional identity. Also, depending on how host people respond to the sojourners' ascribed identities, the weightings of a sojourner's identities (e.g., national vs. regional) may shift from context to context. Their degrees of willingness to communicate, language/intercultural attitudes, agency, and investment may also change.

While studying/traveling abroad is widely regarded as a critical opportunity for language learning, identity expansion (e.g., a broader persona), and intercultural development (e.g., heightened intercultural awareness), the "myth" that believes that an international experience *alone* automatically leads to these gains has been debunked by contemporary research. Study abroad researchers (e.g., Benson et al., 2013; Howard, 2019; Irie & Ryan, 2015; Jackson, 2018; Mitchell et al., 2015, 2017) have identified a complex mix of individual differences (e.g., language/intercultural attitudes, agency, motivation, self-efficacy) and external factors (e.g., host receptivity, access, housing situation, power relations) that can influence sojourners' identity development and learning outcome to varying degrees (language, academic, cultural, personal, professional, etc.).

Jackson's (2019) case study of Zoe, a New Zealand-bound anthropology major from a Hong Kong university, illustrated the complexity and idiosyncrasy of study abroad learning in the identity and intercultural dimension. This interesting study tracked the participant's evolving attitudes toward the host culture/language and contested identities throughout the exchange experience. Interview data revealed that Zoe's social network evolved from primarily spending time with diverse international students (e.g., roommates) in the beginning of the sojourn, to mainly Asians (predominantly co-nationals who shared the same L1) in the middle of the sojourn, and to spending time mostly on her own toward the end of the exchange. Faced with linguistic challenges in academic and social contexts, the participant opted to have little intercultural engagement. This kind of "bubble" experience resulted in ample missed opportunities for intercultural interaction and identity expansion. Upon her reentry to Hong Kong, she did not appear to develop a higher level of intercultural/sociopragmatic competence or experience a broader, expanded self. Her intercultural disengagement and limited exposure to the host culture led to a heightened sense of belonging to Hong Kong and her preferred identity as a Hong Konger. In her narrative, she felt much closer to Cantonese (L1), perceiving it as her "eyes" and English as "just (my) glasses" (Jackson, 2019, p. 33). As the author observes, the unfolding of Zoe's study abroad experience was affected by multiple individual factors (e.g., language anxiety, lack of self-efficacy and investment) and external factors (e.g., limited exposure/access to host communities of practice). Jackson (2019) calls for research-based pedagogical interventions at strategic intervals to support sojourn learning.

Whitworth (2006) investigated the identity development and L2 socialization of four American students in France, with a particular focus on their agency and access to the host language. Informed by the poststructuralist notion of language socialization (Duff, 2002; Pavlenko, 2002a), this longitudinal study revealed divergent developmental trajectories of the case participants. While some exercised their agentive power and benefited from the access to local communities of practice (e.g., access granted by host families and colleagues) and developed diversified social networks (e.g., joining social activities with French friends), others had difficulties in accessing opportunities and, as a result, "withdrew from the French language and culture" (Whitworth, 2006, p. 176). Whitworth (2006) reminds us that in study abroad contexts, student sojourners might not necessarily have unlimited access to and interactional opportunities with the host culture and people and, in fact, gaining access in the host environment is a "truly complex endeavor" (p. 233) that is mediated by the sojourners' linguistic background, gender, race, and social class (Pavlenko, 2002a).

Sun's (2020) study of Chinese STEM international exchange students in the United States also reveals the complex nature of study abroad learning. Influenced by the dynamic interplay between internal and external factors, some participants did not fully recognize the affordances in the host environment and avoided intercultural interactions in and outside the class (e.g., choosing co-nationals for group work, joining social activities with co-nationals only). Some failed to "unpack" the perceived "negative" intercultural encounters and returned home with reinforced stereotypes of the host culture and people, a heightened ethnocentric mindset, and very little interest in intercultural interaction in the future (Sun, 2020). The findings support contemporary study abroad literature that suggests that identity and intercultural development during study abroad is complex and highly idiosyncratic (Benson et al., 2013; Iwasaki, 2019; Jackson, 2018).

5.4 Workplace

Workplace interaction has been studied by language and intercultural communication scholars (e.g., Holmes, 2017; Komisarof & Zhu, 2016; Marra & Holmes, 2007). Martin and Nakayama (2015) caution us against the traditional Eurocentric, ethnocentric approaches to intercultural (communication) competence and call for a dialectical approach when examining intercultural competence and identity in global workplaces. They emphasize the dynamic nature of culture and cultural identity (Holliday, 2010) and the complexity of workplace interaction that usually involves the negotiation of multiple identities at the same time; the researchers maintain that a dialectical perspective can facilitate a better understanding of the affordances and constraints facing people from different cultural backgrounds (Martin & Nakayama, 2015).

The Language in the Workplace Project team in New Zealand investigated intercultural workplace discourses, one of the focuses being professional and personal identity construction, among others (e.g., humor, politeness) (Holmes, 2017; Marra & Holmes, 2007). Holmes and Riddiford (2010) studied how migrant workers from different cultural backgrounds negotiated complex workplace talk in their attempt to establish a positive professional identity. The two focal case participants, Helena who was originally from Hong Kong and Andrei from Russia, demonstrated their competency in constructing a professional identity with task-oriented, transactional discourse (e.g., using technical jargon). However, when it came to the relational aspects of discourse in the workplace (e.g., small talk, personal talk), Andrei appeared less competent, and his discourse was deemed unacceptable from a New Zealander's perspective. For example, in an informal social interaction with his mentor, his elaborated professional identity construction (e.g., describing previous experience and expertise) exceeded the perceived appropriate amount and was regarded as "inappropriately blowing one's own trumpet" (Holmes & Riddiford, 2010, p. 7). Helena, on the other hand, demonstrated her relational discourse competence by conforming to New Zealand sociopragmatic norms (e.g., self-depreciation). The rich examples in the study show how relational talk can be a challenge for professional migrants in intercultural workplace interaction. Further, the switches between task-oriented talk and social talk, usually with very subtle signaling, could be a challenge for immigrants who follow different sociopragamtic norms. For immigrants who keep their professional self and personal self apart, it may be difficult to achieve a synthesis of the two aspects of their identities in the workplace.

In the context of volunteer work placements, Holmes (2015) studied the intercultural communication experiences of sixteen immigrants who had lived in New Zealand for a period ranging from three months to six years. The immigrants, aged between twenty-six and fifty-five years old, were skilled professionals with diverse cultural backgrounds. From a social constructionist perspective, the researcher investigated the challenges that the immigrants faced and identified the facilitating or constraining factors in workplace communication. In-depth open-ended interviews were conducted with the immigrants, their employers, and coordinators of the program; data were analyzed following Braun and Clarke (2006). The findings showed that the sociopragmatic aspect of language use was a major challenge for the participants, for example, many had difficulties in engaging in small talk during tea breaks and adjusting to receiving praise from the boss. For many of them, unfamiliar verbal and nonverbal communication styles proved challenging. This led to a mismatch between the participants' avowed identities (fluent speakers of English in their home environment) and ascribed identities (incompetent speakers of English in the New Zealand workplace). The critical intercultural encounters experienced by the immigrants not only caused embarrassment and awkwardness in the workplace but also resulted in a sense of detachment and exclusion. According to Holmes (2015), the workshops organized by the program appeared to help the immigrants to better prepare for workplace communication, particularly in forging self-awareness and sensitivity. The author highlights the role of the support from the host environment (e.g., coordinators, mentors) in facilitating immigrants' adjustment. This study offers insights into how powerless individuals (re)negotiate their positionings in the workplace and (re)construct their identities. It shows how ongoing institutional support and access to the host community of practice can enhance immigrants' communication experiences in a culturally diverse workplace.

Focusing on workplace virtual communication, Lockwood (2015) conducted a case study of the communication practices of international teams at a multinational financial company. With the aim to develop a "communicating in virtual teams" training program, the researcher conducted training needs analysis (TNA) through administering surveys, conducting interviews, reviewing documents, and observing team meetings. The study reported that language and (inter)cultural misunderstandings occurred between offshore staff and their onshore counterparts (e.g., differing perceptions of "silence" in team meetings, (mis)understandings of idioms and accents). The onshore participants revealed more positive attitudes toward team communication and intercultural behaviors (Lockwood, 2015). Offshore participants, on the other hand, expressed frustration and feelings of marginalization in virtual team meetings dominated by onshore managers. Such tension prompted the participants to (re)negotiate their multiple identities in the workplace (e.g., professional, gendered, social) that transcend their national identities. The findings draw our attention to the role of the power differentials (e.g., unequal power relations between onshore and offshore staff) and professional identity struggles faced by staff in intercultural and international workplaces. The findings of the study offer useful insight into intercultural training or intervention program design and implementation in facilitating virtual team communication.

Chan and Du-Babcock (2019) investigated intercultural communication in business meetings from the perspective of leadership behavior. The researchers maintained that an essentialist "culture as nation" perspective adopted in many studies fails to uncover the complexity and diversity of leadership styles in actual practices. Drawing on the theory of communities of practice (Wenger, 1998), the authors examined two authentic meetings in a Finnish–Swedish corporation. Both meetings had Swedish leaders as chairs and the participants came from diverse backgrounds (e.g., Finnish, German). Adopting a microanalytic approach, the researchers analyzed episodes of turn allocation, agenda management, and task assignment to examine how the leaders "did" leadership discursively. The findings showed that a leadership identity was constructed differently by the two chairs who shared the same Swedish national identity. First, the two leaders displayed different orientations toward relational and transactional aspects of leadership (Holmes et al., 2011). The two meeting groups also had different attitudes toward the power dimension in the workplace, with one meeting group being more tolerant of power asymmetries than the other. Interestingly, the researchers observed a restricted turn-taking system that was recognized and approved by team members. The study showed that while some leadership behaviors conformed to what was expected in Swedish culture (e.g., egalitarian leadership style), some did not (e.g., authoritarian leadership style). The authors concluded that doing leadership in intercultural business meetings is a dynamic, complex, and collaborative practice; it is co-constructed by leaders and team members and may not conform to national cultural stereotypes or communicative norms (Chan & Du-Babcock, 2019).

Zooming in on workplace interaction in a Japanese context, Moody (2019) investigated the experiences of American student interns at a Japanese engineering company. Informed by an interactional sociolinguistics approach (Gumperz, 1999), the researcher collected data through site visits and interviews, and audio-recorded the participants' workplace interaction mediated in the host language (i.e., Japanese). The experiences of two case participants, David and Ethan, were presented to illustrate the relationship between identity, humor, and inclusiveness in the intercultural workplace. The findings show that the interns' micro-level linguistic identities and identities related to cultural practices appeared prominent in their interactions with Japanese colleagues. Teasing that is potentially aggressive can serve as a solidarity-building strategy between the locals and the American interns (Moody, 2019). In an intercultural interaction at lunch, David was teased by a Japanese male colleague as an "chopstick amateur" and jokingly teased back by asking if he could pick up beans using chopsticks, making other colleagues laugh. Moody (2019) points out that such potentially face-threatening speech acts about cultural differences actually created "a space for affiliative laughter" (p. 154) that challenged macro-level ideologies. Similarly, self-deprecating remarks from the interns (e.g., claiming that they had difficulty speaking Japanese) created a humorous effect that facilitated intercultural professional relationship building. This study illustrates how humor playing on differences in linguistic and cultural aspects of identities can help to construct a "localized type of inclusiveness" (p. 157) in a Japanese workplace setting.

Situated in the context of Qatar, Al-Khulaifi and Van De Mieroop (2022) took a social constructionist approach to identities and studied the experiences of a native minority group, Qatari female junior academics at a reformed national university. Drawing on membership categorization analysis (MCA), the researchers interviewed twelve female academics who had either obtained or were in the process of obtaining an international master's or doctoral degree. The stories of three focal case participants showed that "othering" strategies were frequently used in the construction and negotiation of identities in the intercultural workplace. For example, when discussing the content in condolence emails from the university, an interviewee positioned the expats working at the university as "foreigners" and "not Qataris" (p. 6). In another discussion on the level of commitment toward the university and interest in the pre-oil-boom Qatar, a participant labeled expat employees as materialistic and her in-groups (native junior academics) as "not materially oriented" (p. 7). An "us versus them" discourse was used to single out "non-Qatari male" as a representative migrant out-group. To be specific, the "mobile migrants" were negatively labeled as materially driven "they/them," whereas "we/us" native in-groups were favorably positioned as noble, loyal to the university and the country.

In Al-Khulaifi and Van De Mieroop's (2022) study, ethnicity appeared evident in the participants' identity construction/negotiation in the workplace. The interview data showed that ethnic identities were foregrounded in almost all intercultural incidents presented in the study. Ethnicity-related strategies of otherization were practiced. Non-Qatari migrant out-groups (e.g., white Europeans) were negatively evaluated by the Qatari native in-groups. Interestingly, as the researchers note, those evaluations were not explicitly linked to the out-groups' work performances, nor their professional capabilities. The authors argue that the otherization strategies can be understood as coping strategies adopted by the female junior academics to "carve out a morally superior position" (p. 13) in their resistance to out-group dominance in the workplace. The authors call for reflections on the institutional reform process to further address the unequal power relations that can marginalize all groups on campus.

5.5 Online Spaces

By connecting people across national and local boundaries, online spaces have become significant sites of identity negotiation and intercultural communication (Darvin, 2022b; Papacharissi, 2010), and within these networked publics (boyd, 2011), users negotiate diverse online cultures, ideologies, and relations of power. In the twentieth anniversary special issue of *Language and Intercultural Communication* that highlights the field's most pressing challenges, Dooly and Darvin (2022) note how digital mediation can shape and amplify processes of social fragmentation and exclusion in often invisible ways. Recognizing how the design and algorithms of digital platforms can construct echo chambers that intensify shared views and diminish ideological opposition, they assert that users need to develop an online intercultural communicative competence that involves a more critical understanding of online interactions. Drawing on the affordances of digital technologies while engaging a critical lens enables not only the agentive performance of identities but also transformative digital practices (Darvin, 2020).

In a case study of a Chinese immigrant teenager living in the United States, Lam (2000) uses ethnographic and discourse analytic methods to examine identity construction online. Through thick description, the researcher illustrates how Almon created a J-pop website that enabled him to interact with a global community of Asians including those in Hong Kong, Japan, Malaysia, the United States, and Canada. Lam discusses how the participant is able to represent and reposition identity through the composition of texts that respond to his relationship with different cultural communities. In a later article, Lam (2004) demonstrates the translingual practices of two teenage Chinese immigrants in the United States in a bilingual chatroom. Through a mixed code of English and romanized Cantonese, the teenagers are able to "create a collective ethnic identity" (p. 44), while using English in specific ways to navigate the locality of the nation-state and online environments.

Another example of the online construction of identities can be found in Thorne and Black's (2011) study of Nanako, an English language learner, on an online fan fiction site. Thorne and Black demonstrate how composing and posting online fan fiction can provide learners with new opportunities for learning and performing identities. By appropriating and integrating popular cultural and linguistic resources to construct fan fiction texts and by interacting with a diverse group who shared a common interest in anime or Japanese animation, Nanako was able to get feedback on her writing and demonstrate her knowledge of Chinese and Japanese language and culture. This dynamic enabled her to negotiate identities of novice and expert while affirming her Asian identity and knowledge of Asian culture as capital. To frame their analysis, Thorne and Black focus on the conditions and affordances mobilized in the digitally mediated context. These are set against three dynamics in internet-mediated interactions: indexical linkages to macro-level categories (ethnic or nation-state affiliations); functionally defined subject positions (e.g., youth, author, expert, novice), and fluid shifts in language choice, stance, and style. By analyzing these interactions, they assert how language development in these online spaces is interlinked with the construction of identities.

Research on identity and interculturality online has also included studies of language teachers. Dooly (2011) followed a year-long telecollaborative exchange that took place between student teachers in Barcelona, Spain, and Illinois, in the United States. Utilizing online communicative tools (e.g., Moodle, Skype), the two groups of student teachers formed working groups, provided feedback on their peers' teaching unit designs, and co-developed a podcast activity suitable for a face-to-face instructional setting. At the end of the telecollaborative exchange, both groups appeared to become more reflective and more critical of their own and their peers' teaching practices. In the virtual space, they gradually adopted the "ways of doing" of a teacher (e.g., using jargon) and constructed a professional teacher identity. Coming from diverse cultural and linguistic backgrounds, the participants in the teacher training program were able to engage in meaningful interaction through constructing a shared teacher identity in a "third space" that transcends cultural boundaries. In a digitalized "third space," Dooly (2011) urges us to reconsider what "intercultural" could mean, and what intercultural communicative competence could entail in a space that requires knowledge, skills, and competencies that may transcend cultural borders in the "real," offline world (Dooly, 2011).

Focusing on the multimodal aspects of intercultural communication, Ho (2022) investigated how interculturality is constructed by microcelebrities in an online space. The study focused on Teacher Mike, a YouTube celebrity American English teacher living in China, who returned to the United States during the COVID-19 pandemic. Two "moments" of his interaction with staff members in a Chinese supermarket in the United States were selected for detailed multimodal analysis. Drawing on a range of linguistic and semiotic resources (e.g., interacting with staff members), the celebrity teacher adopted multiple cultural positions (e.g., aligning toward Chinese culture) to perform his avowed identities (e.g., someone who has spent many years in China and understands Chinese language and culture). The study illustrates the "strategic orchestration of multilingual and multimodal resources" (Ho, 2022, p. 663) in the construction of multiple identities. Ho (2022) argues that interculturality and identity construction in online spaces is not only discursive but multimodal.

With a similar focus on online microcelebrities, Shi and colleagues (2022) studied the identity construction of transnational microcelebrities on the Chinese video-sharing website *Bilibili*. Informed by Darvin and Norton's (2015) model of investment, the researchers focused on three American content creators on *Bilibili* to examine how invested they were in the construction of a transnational identity. A total of 212 videos were collected for content analysis; seven themes were generated from the dataset. The findings show that the three microcelebrities were able to gain legitimate membership of the Chinese online community by investing in Chinese language/cultural practices, relationship building with followers, sharing insider perspectives of American culture, and demonstrating knowledge as intercultural/global citizens (Shi et al., 2022). By performing transnational identities, the content creators utilized multiple affordances (e.g., bilingual, professional, multimodal) to negotiate power, and ultimately gained legitimacy in this digital space.

By discussing contemporary identity research that involves intercultural communication, this section demonstrates how identity can be a generative theoretical lens through which to examine contexts of language learning and teaching, migration, and study abroad and traveling abroad, together with workplace settings and online spaces. It provides a deeper understanding of how identity construction is imbricated with both material and symbolic considerations, such as agency, sociopragmatic awareness, gender, power relations, and access to the host language/culture, and so on, impacting the negotiation of identities in various intercultural contexts.

6 Researching Identity

One fundamental challenge in identity research is that no matter how meticulously it is executed and articulated across spatiotemporal scales, it will always be partial (Block, 2010). Given that identity is constructed through discourse, researchers will need to continually grapple with how many interviews, stories, and artifacts can sufficiently represent an individual's identity. Aligned with a social constructionist view of intercultural communication, identity research pays attention to the micro-level of interaction and meaning making while recognizing how utterances can index institutional constraints and modes of exclusion. To develop insights into the complex ways identity is performed, researchers adopt, modify, and design methodologies that fit their specific purposes, and this section lists some popular methodologies in terms of researching identity and their corresponding issues.

6.1 Ethnography

Brewer (2000) defines ethnography as "the study of people in naturally occurring settings or 'fields' by means of methods which capture their social meanings and ordinary activities, involving the researcher participating directly in the setting, if not also the activities, in order to collect data in a systematic manner but without meaning being imposed on them externally" (p. 10).

Through this on-the-ground observation, intercultural communication researchers can gain an awareness of why people act, think, and feel the way they do in specific situations and how aspects of identity are made salient (Wacquant, 2003). While ethnographers can be active participants, privileged observers, or limited observers (Wolcott, 2008), they observe and document cultural or behavioral practices in order to understand the meanings that people attach to such practices, and the way they position themselves and others. As such, culture is at the centre of ethnographic research, as it accounts for social activity from which cultural patterning can be discerned (Wolcott, 2008).

Jackson (2015) identifies specific features of ethnography: a focus on a specific group or cultural scene in a natural setting; a holistic investigation of a sociocultural phenomenon with particular attention to behavior and language use. Data can be collected through participant observation, interviewing, ethnographic conversations, focus groups, videotaping, and analysis of artifacts like diaries/ journals and visual materials. In analyzing data, researchers are also expected to exercise reflexivity, "the process of reflecting critically on the self as researcher, the 'human as instrument'" (Lincoln & Guba, 2000, p. 183) or "turning back on oneself" (Davies, 2008, p. 4) so that they can acknowledge and explain their biases, social positions, worldviews, and lived experiences that can impact their research. Recognizing how poststructuralist concerns have implications for ethnographic representation, Britzman (1995) proposes ways of writing poststructural ethnography that disrupt the cohesiveness of identity and the seamlessness of narrative, providing a space for contradictory interpretations and different regimes of truth.

6.2 Case Study

As a research approach, the case study approach has generally provided a contextualized profile of a person or a cultural group, for example, Italian Americans or Chinese study abroad students in the UK. Case studies analyze linguistic, cultural, and social phenomena to understand individuals' intercultural experiences within specific contexts. There are some case studies, as part of mixed-methods research designs, that analyze both quantitatively measured linguistic dimensions of interactions and qualitatively described sociocultural dimensions (e.g., Duff et al., 2013; Kinginger, 2008). A great number of recently published case studies in applied linguistics though have foregrounded personal and sociocultural aspects of lived experiences without detailed linguistic descriptions (see Darvin, 2017 for an example). This emerging body of research examines the shifting identities of language learners at different life stages, using diverse repertoires, while constrained by norms, ideologies, and policies (Duff, 2014).

While the case study approach is able to provide a better understanding of the context and processes of a phenomenon, it has often been caught in a methodological crossfire because of a number of issues. These include questions of what one can generalize on the basis of an individual case and how such a case contains a bias toward verification or a tendency to confirm the researcher's preconceived ideas (Flyvbjerg, 2011). Flyvbjerg (2011) challenges these "misunderstandings" by pointing out that even the scientific conclusions of Newton, Einstein, and Darwin were based on carefully chosen cases and that the case study approach contains no greater bias than other methods of inquiry that also involve the subjective judgments of the researcher. The number of cases and the length of time a study is conducted may be debatable, but Duff (2014) argues these decisions can be made based on the research topic and the number of candidates who agree to participate. By making sound methodological decisions, identity researchers, through the case study approach, are able to cast a light on the complexity and contradictions of individuals and to find generalizable connections.

6.3 Narrative Inquiry

Canagarajah (1996) asserts that narratives are able to represent knowledge "from the bottom up" (p. 327) and have the powerful potential to represent in a comprehensive and more open-ended way the identities of research participants. As a systematic study and interpretation of stories of life experiences, narrative inquiry has become a popular research approach in applied linguistics (Barkhuizen, 2008, 2010; Bell, 2002; Pavlenko, 2002b, 2007). One specific approach to narrative inquiry is highlighting the "identity work" research participants engage in "as they construct selves within specific institutional, organizational, discursive and local cultural contexts" (Chase, 2005, p. 658). In a study that examined researcher identity, Norton and Early (2011) draw on Bamberg's (2006) conception of big stories that focus on life histories and small stories that are centered on small talk and regular conversation. They reflect that while small stories-in-interaction may not create a coherent sense of self, they can highlight the diverse identities that one performs in everyday interactive practices.

One of the challenges of narrative researchers is to understand what is "story worthy" in the participant's social setting and to orient to the particularity of their story and voice (Chase, 2005). Pavlenko (2007) identifies a number of issues of narrative research that are linked to content and thematic analysis. The lack of both a theoretical premise and a set of established procedures, she argues, obscures how conceptual categories are identified and linked to specific instances. The focus on what recurs in the text can also lead to the oversight of important events that need not have happened repeatedly and of the gaps and absences in a text that are themselves meaningful. The most problematic issue, however, Pavlenko points out, is the lack of attention to how narratives are constructed through carefully chosen language. In this case, storytellers use words that position them in specific ways and reflect their own interpretive stances.

6.4 Conversation Analysis

Benwell and Stokoe (2006) assert that while conversation analysts do not usually begin with identity as a theoretical tool, they recognize that social life is grounded in interaction and constituted by talk. Identities are made relevant by conversational participants and are constructed in sequence. If ethnomethodologists and conversation analysts were to adopt a theory on identity therefore, it would be an "indexical, context bound theory, in which identity is understood as an oriented-to, recipient-designed accomplishment of inter-action" (p. 68). Research thus has to begin with an analysis of identity categor-ies that is not based on what analysts take to be relevant but on what people do and say as they deploy categories. Conversation analysis (CA) collects naturally occurring data where participants proceed with their daily routines. This means, however, that there is low standardization and comparability at the level of the interaction (Kasper & Wagner, 2014).

In a study of how the identity of "ESL student" is constructed in routine classroom interactions between students and the teacher, Talmy (2009) demon-strates how CA can be productive in critical research on the way learners are positioned. By grounding theories of language socialization and cultural pro-duction in the participants' discursive practices, he asserts that CA can provide an analytic frame that shows how power is achieved in interaction before any a priori conclusion. By examining language at work, the researcher of identity can investigate how biases and assumptions of race, ethnicity, or class are "instantiated, resisted, accommodated, reproduced, and/or transformed" (p. 206) in daily routines and activities. For Kasper and Wagner (2014), one of the greatest advantages of CA is that it offers researchers a coherent, inte-grated theory and methodology of interactions to investigate language-related real-life problems. Social problem-oriented CA examines how power imbal-ances are constructed through interactional practices in various settings like courtrooms or hospitals, positioning speakers by virtue of their situated iden-tities. Kasper and Wagner point out that while CA in its earlier stages was limited by an entrenched monolingualism, more recent research has rectified this through studies that focus on the practices of multilingual interaction (He, 2013; Higgins, 2009; Li, 2011; Nevile & Wagner, 2011).

6.5 Critical Discourse Analysis

Predicated on the idea that discursive and social processes are woven together, critical discourse analysis (CDA) offers identity researchers a framework to examine how identity constructions are circumscribed by power relations and ideology. By critiquing unequal social practices, CDA demonstrates how the social positions of individuals allow them differential access to linguistic, cultural, and economic capital and varying degrees of recognition. It draws attention to contextual constraints and affordances that influence the projected and ascribed identities of people (Zotzmann & O'Regan, 2016). Cheng (2013) points out that a great number of CDA studies in the past two decades have examined media and political discourses and that CDA would benefit from exploring more diverse text types. With the rise of digital media, there has also been a greater need for multimodal analytical tools that take into account new genres and formats to examine super-diverse and super-vernacular texts (Lin, 2014).

Recognizing that discourses about social groups are reproduced by structures of power, Escamilla (2013) uses CDA to examine how Japanese mainstream news media constructs the identity of *gaikokujin* or resident foreign nationals, particularly ethnically Japanese Brazilians who back-migrated to Japan. Drawing on a corpus of thirty-six articles from regional and national news platforms, he analyzes how lexical choices contribute to the othering and deauthentication of these foreign nationals. In this case, CDA enables the examination of how public discourse can construct minority identity and reinforce dominant cultural assumptions (Belcher & Nelson, 2013). Because identity is itself a discursive phenomenon, CDA uses language as a way to understand how identities are formed, represented, and enacted in unequal ways. Although it does not have a homogeneous theoretical framework or a set of fixed methodological tools, its commitment to a critique of inequitable social practices is geared toward contributing to greater transformative action (Zotzmann & O'Regan, 2016).

6.6 Digital Ethnography

As the digital becomes more embedded in everyday life, researchers are confronted with a more complex array of potential sites and sources of data. Tying together disparate insights from diverse digital practices to understand identity production becomes a more complex task. Hine (2015) talks about the need for an "ethnography of an embedded, embodied, everyday Internet" (p. 56) where researchers are able to move between face-to-face to mediated forms of interaction, challenging the notion of conventionally bounded field sites and allowing a multi-sited field to emerge. This connective, itinerant, or networked ethnography requires an openness to exploring connections as they present themselves. Leander (2008) defines connective ethnography as a methodological approach "that considers connections and relations as normative social practices and Internet social spaces as connected to other social spaces" (p. 37). Recognizing the connectedness of these spaces, Büscher and Urry (2009) have devised mobile methods that allow researchers to examine these online and offline practices through the frame of movement. In this case, data collection takes into account the bodily travel of people and virtual travel across networks, as people are connected in face-to-face interactions and via mediated communications. Recognizing differences between synchronous and asynchronous social media communication, Dovchin (2019) conducted digital ethnographies of university students in Mongolia and Japan using Facebook to understand how their performance of identities shaped their translingual practices online.

Hine (2015) points out that a number of issues arise when a field site extends to the online realm. While ethnographers emphasize immersion in a setting as a means of knowledge generation, an ethnography of the Internet raises questions about how to define prolonged immersion and how to determine the boundaries of limitless online space. New issues of privacy and confidentiality also arise when researchers gain access to the social media accounts of participants. Researchers become perpetually present, and participants need to decide which social media activities they want to provide access to (Baker, 2013; Eynon et al., 2008). Not only does this require continual negotiation through informed consent but it also involves participants actively managing their privacy settings. At the same time, for ethnographers to access and observe the social media activities of participants on sites like X (formerly Twitter) or Facebook, they need to make themselves present by adding or friending them. Researchers become more visible, and this requires them to make informed decisions about how to manage their own online identities.

7 Conclusion

In a globalized world characterized by mobility, fluidity, and diversity, the dynamics of intercultural communication have become more complex, requiring theoretical tools that reject essentialist notions of culture and language. Drawing on a poststructural and critical lens, this Element has demonstrated how identity can serve as a generative construct to address this need, examined alongside notions of indexicality, positionality, and intersectionality. Constructed through discourse, identity is always contextualized, situated, and performed, and it enables us to dissect intercultural encounters and the ways speakers position themselves and are positioned by others. By recognizing how race, ethnicity, nationality, and class are made relevant by interlocutors in these encounters, identity casts a light on different relations of power. As speakers negotiate their resources, whether it be in intercultural contexts of language learning and teaching, migration, study abroad, workplaces, or online communication, identity needs to be understood as a process, as something performed and ongoing, and circumscribed by different inequalities. It is through such an approach that identity research can contribute to a critical and transformative understanding of intercultural communication.

Recognizing the fluidity and intersectionality of identity, however, poses a number of challenges in the way critical intercultural communication research can be conducted. One challenge is finding ways to resist immediately imposing identity inscriptions on research participants at the onset of a study, especially as this involves identifying research populations and formulating research questions without making a priori assumptions about which categories would be relevant. If identity is continually constructed by speakers in specific situations through discourse, determining the theoretical parameters that would constitute a coherent study becomes challenging. To examine issues of power and inequality, researchers will need to master strategies of dissecting utterances not only to make visible the identity inscriptions made relevant in specific situations but also to trace how these utterances index ideologies and relations and structures of power. Conducting such an analysis involves negotiating this "layered simultaneity" (Blommaert, 2005, p. 130), and recognizing that while discourse occurs in real time, it is also encapsulated in several layers of historicity. Rudolph (2023) asserts that apart from resisting the essentialization of participant identities, critical researchers also need to avoid falling into the trap of homogenizing contexts and essentializing the discourses of power they are trying to undo. This extended criticality involves problematizing further the binaries embedded in conceptualizations of privilege and marginalization, that is, white, male, heterosexual, Western ways of knowing that are juxtaposed against otherness. Given the complexities of how inequalities are both experienced and examined, researchers will need to exercise greater reflexivity to understand how their own identities can shape the way they interpret these interactions (Consoli & Ganassin, 2023), and to ensure they do not reproduce processes of othering and objectifying research subjects (Dervin & Risager, 2015).

For identity to continue being a generative construct in critical intercultural communication, researchers need analytical tools that can help dissect the layered simultaneity of discourse in order to make connections between the situated and the systemic. Recognizing how speakers move across online/ offline spaces with greater fluidity, Darvin and Norton's (2015) model of investment draws attention to how dispositions, practices, and desires are shaped not only by lived experiences but also by institutional structures and patterns of control. Proposing the notion of transcultural communication to better signal the fluidity of communicative practices, Baker (2022) recommends a scalar approach (Canagarajah & De Costa, 2016) to analyze multilingual situations without making a priori characterizations of languages used in interaction. Aligned with Lam and Christiansen's (2022) chronotopic analysis discussed in an earlier section, this approach highlights how multiple spatiotemporal scales can be simultaneously present in discourse and enables an understanding of how identity is discursively constructed and historically produced. A greater attention to indexicality is not only a way to move the field forward into a more critical domain, but also to participate in the project of decolonization (Dei, 2019). By understanding how intercultural encounters index historically and socially reproduced inequalities, identity researchers can make visible how colonialism and Eurocentric epistemologies (Darvin & Zhang, 2023) have constructed formations of race and ethnicity (Motha, 2020) and the compartmentalization of languages and cultures (Darvin, 2022a; Tupas, 2019). Expanding the subjects of normative lines of study to understand further ways of being and doing of Indigenous peoples, rural folk, and members of the Global South (Pennycook & Makoni, 2019) not only broadens our understanding of the inequalities of a globalized world, but also provides us opportunities to integrate more diverse forms of knowledge in the study of language and intercultural communication.

References

Al-Khulaifi, A., & Van De Mieroop, D. (2022). Othering the expat majority: Qatari junior academics' identity work at the interface of migration and institutional reform. *Language and Intercultural Communication*,1–16. https://doi.org/10.1080/14708477.2022.2090572.

Anderson, B. (1991). *Imagined communities: Reflections on the origin and spread of nationalism* (2nd ed.). Verso.

Anya, U. (2011). Connecting with communities of learners and speakers: Integrative ideals, experiences, and motivations of successful black second language learners. *Foreign Language Annals, 44*(3), 441–466.

Anya, U. (2017). *Speaking blackness in Brazil: Racialized identities in second language learning*. Routledge.

Appadurai, A. (1990). Disjuncture and difference in the global cultural economy. *Theory, Culture and Society, 7*(2–3), 295–310.

Appleby, R. (2013). Desire in translation: White masculinity and TESOL. *TESOL Quarterly, 47*(1), 122–147.

Atkinson, D. (1999). TESOL and culture. *TESOL Quarterly, 3*(3), 625–654.

Baker, S. (2013). Conceptualising the use of Facebook in ethnographic research: As tool, as data and as context. *Ethnography and Education, 8*, 131–145.

Baker, W. (2015). *Culture and identity through English as a lingua franca*. De Gruyter Mouton.

Baker, W. (2022). From intercultural to transcultural communication. *Language and Intercultural Communication, 22*(3), 280–293.

Bakhtin, M. M. (1981). *The dialogic imagination: Four essays* (C. Emerson & M. Holquist, Trans.). University of Texas Press.

Bamberg, M. (2006). Stories: Big or small: Why do we care? *Narrative Inquiry, 16*, 139–147.

Barkhuizen, G. (2008). A narrative approach to exploring context in language teaching. *English Language Teaching Journal, 62*, 231–239.

Barkhuizen, G. (2010). An extended positioning analysis of a pre-service teacher's better life small story. *Applied Linguistics, 31*, 282–300.

Barkhuizen, G. (Ed.) (2017). *Reflections on language teacher identity research*. Routledge.

Barkhuizen, G. (2021). *Language teacher educator identity*. Cambridge University Press.

Barton, D., & Lee, C. (2013). *Language online: Investigating digital texts and practices*. Routledge.

Basch, L., Schiller, N., & Blanc, C. (1994). *Nations unbound: Transnational projects, postcolonial predicaments and deterritorialized nation-states.* Gordon and Breach.

Baumann, G. (1996). *Contesting culture: Discourses of identity in multi-ethnic London.* Cambridge University Press.

Belcher, D., & Nelson, G. (2013). Why intercultural rhetoric needs critical and corpus-based approaches: An introduction. In D. Belcher & G. Nelson (Eds.), *Critical and corpus-based approaches to intercultural rhetoric* (pp. 1–6). University of Michigan Press.

Bell, J. S. (2002). Narrative inquiry: More than just telling stories. *TESOL Quarterly, 36*, 207–213.

Benson, P., Barkhuizen, G., Bodycott, P., & Brown, J. (2013). *Second language identity in narratives of study abroad.* Palgrave Macmillan.

Benwell, B., & Stokoe, L. (2006) *Discourse and identity.* Edinburgh University Press.

Block, D. (2010). Researching language and identity. In B. Paltridge & A. Phakiti (Eds.), *Continuum companion to research methods in applied linguistics* (pp. 337–349). Continuum.

Block, D. (2012). Class and SLA: Making connections. *Language Teaching Research, 16*(2), 188–205.

Block, D. (2013). The structure and agency dilemma in identity and intercultural communication research. *Language and Intercultural Communication, 13*(2), 126–147.

Block, D. (2022). *Innovations and challenges in identity research.* Routledge.

Block, D., & Corona, V. (2014). Exploring class-based intersectionality. *Language, Culture and Curriculum, 27*(1), 27–42.

Blommaert, J. (2005). *Discourse: A critical introduction.* Cambridge University Press.

Blommaert, J. (2007) Sociolinguistics and discourse analysis: Orders of indexicality and polycentricity. *Journal of Multicultural Discourses, 2*(2), 115–130.

Blommaert, J., & Rampton, B. (2011). Language and superdiversity. *Diversities, 13*(2), 1–21.

Bourdieu, P. (1990). *The logic of practice.* Stanford University Press.

boyd, D. (2011). Social network sites as networked publics: Affordances, dynamics, and implications. In Z. Papacharissi (Ed.), *A networked self: Identity, community and culture* (pp. 39–58). Routledge.

boyd, D. (2014). *It's complicated: The social lives of networked teens.* Yale University Press.

Braun, V., & Clarke, V. (2006). Using thematic analysis in psychology. *Qualitative Research in Psychology*, *3*, 77–101. https://doi.org/10.1191/1478088706qp 063oa.

Brewer, J. (2000). *Ethnography*. Open University Press.

Britzman, D. P. (1995). "The question of belief": Writing poststructural ethnography. *Qualitative Studies in Education*, *8*(3), 229–238.

Bucher, T. (2018). *If . . . then: Algorithmic power and politics*. Oxford University Press.

Bucholtz, M. (2004). Styles and stereotypes: The linguistic negotiation of identity among Laotian American youth. *Pragmatics*, *14*(2–3), 127–147.

Burr, V. (2015). *Social constructionism* (3rd ed.). Routledge.

Büscher, M., & Urry, J. (2009). Mobile methods and the empirical. *European Journal of Social Theory*, *12*(1), 99–116.

Butler, J. (1990). *Gender trouble: Feminism and the subversion of identity*. Routledge.

Canagarajah, S. (1996). From critical research practice to critical research reporting. *TESOL Quarterly*, *30*, 321–331.

Canagarajah, S. (2013). *Literacy as translingual practice: Between communities and classrooms*. Routledge.

Canagarajah, S., & De Costa, P. (2016). Introduction: Scales analysis, and its uses and prospects in educational linguistics. *Linguistics and Education*, *34*, 1–10.

Chan, A. C., & Du-Babcock, B. (2019). Leadership in action: An analysis of leadership behaviour in intercultural business meetings. *Language and Intercultural Communication*, 19(2), 201–216. https://doi.org/10.1080/14708477.2018.1508291.

Chase, S. (2005). Narrative inquiry: Multiple lenses, approaches, voices. In N. Denzin & Y. Lincoln (Eds.), *The SAGE handbook of qualitative research* (3rd ed., pp. 651–680). SAGE.

Cheng, W. (2013). Corpus-based linguistic approaches to critical discourse analysis. In C. Chapelle (Ed.), *The encyclopedia of applied linguistics* (pp. 1353–1360). John Wiley.

Clarke M. A. (2019). Creating contexts for teacher development. In S. Walsh & S. Mann (Eds.), *The Routledge handbook of English language teacher education* (pp. 365–382). Routledge.

Consoli, S., & Ganassin, S. (2023). *Reflexivity in applied linguistics: Opportunities, challenges and suggestions*. Routledge.

Curtis, A., & Romney, M. (2006). *Color, race, and English language teaching: Shades of meaning*. Lawrence Erlbaum.

Darvin, R. (2017). Social class and the inequality of English speakers in a globalized world. *Journal of English as a Lingua Franca, 6*(2), 287–311.

Darvin, R. (2020). Creativity and criticality: Reimagining narratives through translanguaging and transmediation. *Applied Linguistics Review, 11*(4), 581–606.

Darvin, R. (2022a). TikTok and the translingual practices of Filipino domestic workers in Hong Kong. *Discourse, Context & Media, 50,* 100655.

Darvin, R. (2022b). Design, resistance and the performance of identity on TikTok. *Discourse, Context & Media, 46,* 100591.

Darvin, R. (2023). Sociotechnical structures, materialist semiotics, and online language learning. *Language Learning & Technology, 27*(2), 28–45. https://hdl.handle.net/10125/73502.

Darvin, R., & Norton, B. (2014). Transnational identity and migrant language learners: The promise of digital storytelling. *Education Matters: The Journal of Teaching and Learning, 2*(1).

Darvin, R., & Norton, B. (2015). Identity and a model of investment in applied linguistics. *Annual Review of Applied Linguistics, 35,* 36–55.

Darvin, R., & Zhang, Y. (2023). Words that don't translate: Investing in decolonizing practices through translanguaging. *Language Awareness,* 1–17. https://doi.org/10.1080/09658416.2023.2238595.

Davies, B., & Harré, R. (1990). Positioning: The discursive production of selves. *Journal for the Theory of Social Behaviour, 20*(1), 43–63.

Davies, C. A. (2008). *Reflexive ethnography: A guide to researching selves and others* (2nd ed.). Routledge.

De Costa, P. I. (2010). Reconceptualizing language, language learning, and the adolescent immigrant language learner in the age of postmodern globalization. *Language and Linguistics Compass, 4*(9), 769–781.

De Fina, A. (2007). Code-switching and the construction of ethnic identity in a community of practice. *Language in Society, 36,* 371–392.

Dei, G. (2019). Decolonizing education for inclusivity: Implications for literacy education. In K. Magro & M. Honeyford (Eds.), *Transcultural literacies: Re-visioning relations in teaching and learning* (pp. 5–29). Canadian Scholars' Press.

Dervin, F., & Risager, K. (Eds.) (2015). *Researching identity and interculturality.* Routledge.

Dooly, M. A. (2011). Crossing the intercultural borders into 3rd space culture-(s): Implications for teacher education in the twenty-first century. *Language and Intercultural Communication, 11*(4), 319–337.

Dooly, M. A., & Darvin, R. (2022). Intercultural communicative competence in the digital age: Critical digital literacy and inquiry-based pedagogy.

Language and Intercultural Communication, 22(3), 354–366. https://doi.org/10.1080/14708477.2022.2063304.

Dörnyei, Z. (2009). The L2 motivational self system. In Z. Dörnyei & E. Ushioda (Eds.), *Motivation, language identity and the L2 self* (pp. 9–42). Bristol : Multilingual Matters.

Dörnyei, Z., & Ushioda, E. (Eds.). (2009). *Motivation, language identities and the L2 self.* Multilingual Matters.

Dovchin, S. (2019). *Language, social media and ideologies: Translingual Englishes, Facebook and authenticities.* Springer.

Duchêne, A., & Heller, M. (Eds.). (2012). *Language in late capitalism: Pride and profit* (Vol. 1). Routledge.

Duff, P. A. (2002). The discursive co-construction of knowledge, identity, and difference: An ethnography of communication in the high school mainstream. *Applied Linguistics, 23*(3), 289–322.

Duff, P. A. (2014). Case study research on language learning and use. *Annual Review of Applied Linguistics, 34*, 233–255.

Duff, P., Anderson, T., Ilnyckyj, R., Van Gaya, E., Wang, R., & Yates, E. (2013). *Learning Chinese: Linguistic, sociocultural, and narrative perspectives.* De Gruyter.

Elliott, A., & Urry, J. (2010). *Mobile lives.* Routledge.

Escamilla, R. (2013). Discriminatory discursive strategies used by the Japanese mainstream news media in constructing the identity of resident foreign nationals: A critical discourse analysis-based examination. In D. Belcher & G. Nelson (Eds.), *Critical and corpus-based approaches to intercultural rhetoric* (pp. 72–96). University of Michigan Press.

Eynon, R., Fry, J., & Schroeder, R. (2008). The ethics of internet research. In N. Fielding, R. Lee, & G. Blank (Eds.), *The SAGE handbook of online research methods* (pp. 23–41). SAGE.

Feinauer, E., & Whiting, E. F. (2012). Examining the sociolinguistic context in schools and neighborhoods of pre-adolescent Latino students: Implications for ethnic identity. *Journal of Language, Identity & Education, 11*(1), 52–74.

Flores, N., & Rosa, J. (2015). Undoing appropriateness: Raciolinguistic ideologies and language diversity in education. *Harvard Educational Review, 85*(2), 149–171.

Flyvbjerg, B. (2011). Case study. In N. Denzin & Y. Lincoln (Eds.), *The SAGE handbook of qualitative research* (pp. 301–316). SAGE.

Gardner, R., & Lambert, W. (1972). *Attitudes and motivation in second-language learning.* Newbury.

Giles, H., & Johnson, P. (1987). Ethnolinguistic identity theory: A social psychological approach to language maintenance. *International Journal of the Sociology of Language, 68*, 69–99.

Gillespie, T. (2018). Regulation of and by platforms. In J. Burgess, A. Marwick, & T. Poell (Eds.), *The SAGE handbook of social media* (pp. 254–278). SAGE.

Gu, M. (2018). Teaching students from other cultures: An exploration of language teachers' experiences with ethnic minority students. *Journal of Language, Identity & Education, 17*(1), 1–15. https://doi.org/10.1080/15348458.2017.1381566.

Gu, M., Jiang, L., & Ou, W. (2022). Exploring the professional teacher identity as ethical self-formation of two multilingual native English teachers. *Language Teaching Research*, 1–23. https://doi.org/10.1177/13621688221117061.

Gumperz, J. (1982). *Language and social identity*. Cambridge University Press.

Gumperz, J. J. (1999). Contextualization revisited. In P. Auer & A. Di Luzio (Eds.), *The contextualization of language* (pp. 39–53). John Benjamins.

Gunderson, L. (2007). *English-only instruction and immigrant students in secondary schools: A critical examination*. Mahwah, NJ: Lawrence Erlbaum.

Gupta, A., & Ferguson, J. (Eds.). (1997). *Culture, power, and place: Explorations in critical anthropology*. Duke University Press.

Hall, K., & Bucholtz, M. (Eds.) (1995). *Gender articulated: Language and the socially constructed self*. Routledge.

Hall, S. (1996) Who needs identity? in S. Hall & P. du Gay (Eds.), *Questions of cultural identity* (pp. 1–17). SAGE.

Hall, S. (2012). *Questions of cultural identity*. SAGE.

He, A. W. (2013). The wor(l)d is a collage: Multi-performance by Chinese heritage language speakers. *Modern Language Journal, 97*, 304–317.

Higgins, C. (2009). "Are you Hindu?" Resisting membership categorization through language alternation. In H. Nguyen & G. Kasper (Eds.), *Talk-in-interaction: Multilingual perspectives* (pp. 111–136). University of Hawai'i.

Hine, C. (2015). *Ethnography for the internet: Embedded, embodied and everyday*. Bloomsbury.

HKUPOP (2019). Rift widens between Chinese and Hong Kong identities, national pride plunges to one in four. Hong Kong University Public Opinion Programme (HKUPOP). www.hkupop.hku.hk/english/release/release1594.html.

Ho, W. Y. J. (2022). ""Coming here you should speak Chinese": The multimodal construction of interculturality in YouTube videos. *Language and Intercultural Communication, 22*(6), 1–19. https://doi.org/10.1080/14708477.2022.2056610.

Holland, D., & Lave, J. (Eds.) (2001). *History in person: Enduring struggles, contentious practice, intimate identities.* School of American Research Press.

Holliday, A. (2006). Native-speakerism. *ELT Journal, 60*(4), 385–387.

Holliday, A. (2010). Complexity in cultural identity. *Language and Intercultural Communication, 10*(2), 165–177. https://doi.org/10.1080/14708470903267384.

Holliday, A. (2013). *Understanding intercultural communication: Negotiating a grammar of culture.* Routledge.

Holmes, J. (2017). Intercultural communication in the workplace. *The Routledge handbook of language in the workplace* (pp. 335–347). Routledge.

Holmes, J., Marra, M., & Vine, B. (2011). *Leadership, discourse and ethnicity.* Oxford University Press.

Holmes, J., & Riddiford, N. (2010). Professional and personal identity at work: Achieving a synthesis through intercultural workplace talk. *Journal of Intercultural Communication, 10*(1), 1–17. https://doi.org/10.36923/jicc.v10i1.494.

Holmes, P. (2015). "The cultural stuff around how to talk to people": Immigrants' intercultural communication during a pre-employment work-placement. *Language and Intercultural Communication, 15*(1), 109–124. https://doi.org/10.1080/14708477.2014.985309.

Howard, M. (Ed.). (2019). *Study abroad, second language acquisition and interculturality.* Multilingual Matters.

Humphreys, G., & Baker, W. (2021). Developing intercultural awareness from short-term study abroad: Insights from an interview study of Japanese students. *Language and Intercultural Communication, 21*(2), 260–275. https://doi.org/10.1080/14708477.2020.1860997.

Irie, K., & Ryan, S. (2015). Study abroad and the dynamics of change in learner L2 self-concept. In Z. Dörnyei, P. D. MacIntyre, & A. Henry (Eds.), *Motivational dynamics in language learning* (pp. 343–366). Multilingual Matters.

Iwasaki, N. (2019). Individual differences in study abroad research: Sources, processes and outcomes of students' development in language, culture, and personhood. In M. Howard (Ed.), *Study abroad, second language acquisition and interculturality* (pp. 237–262). Multilingual Matters.

Jackson, J. (2008). *Language, identity, and study abroad: Sociocultural perspectives.* Equinox.

Jackson, J. (2010). *Intercultural journeys: From study to residence abroad.* Palgrave Macmillan.

Jackson, J. (2015). "Unpacking" international experience through blended intercultural praxis. In R. D. Williams & A. Lee (Eds.), *Internationalizing higher education: Critical collaborations across the curriculum* (pp. 231–252). Sense Publishers.

Jackson, J. (2018). *Interculturality in international education.* Routledge.

Jackson, J. (2019). "Cantonese is my own eyes and English is just my glasses": The evolving language attitudes and L2 identities of a Chinese study abroad student. In M. Howard (Ed.), *Study abroad, second language acquisition and interculturality* (pp. 15–45). Multilingual Matters.

Jones, R. H., & Hafner, C. A. (2021). *Understanding digital literacies: A practical introduction* (2nd ed.). Routledge.

Kanno, Y., & Norton, B. (Eds.). (2003). Imagined communities and educational possibilities. *Journal of Language, Identity, and Education, 2*(4), 241–349.

Kasper, G., & Wagner, J. (2014). Conversation analysis in applied linguistics. *Annual Review of Applied Linguistics, 34,* 171–212.

Kelly, P. (2012). Migration, transnationalism and the spaces of class identity. *Philippine Studies: Historical and Ethnographic Viewpoints, 60*(2), 153–186.

Kim, J., & Duff, P. A. (2012). The language socialization and identity negotiations of generation 1.5 Korean-Canadian university students. *TESL Canada Journal, 29,* 81. https://doi.org/10.18806/tesl.v29i0.1111.

Kinginger, C. (2004). Alice doesn't live here anymore: Foreign language learning and identity construction. In A. P avlenko & A. Blackledge (Eds.), *Negotiation of identities in multilingual contexts* (pp. 219–242). Multilingual Matters.

Kinginger, C. (2008). Language learning in study abroad: Case studies of Americans in France. *The Modern Language Journal, 92,* 1–124.

Kinginger, C. (2015). Student mobility and identity-related language learning. *Intercultural Education, 26*(1), 6–15. https://doi.org/10.1080/14675986.2015.992199.

Kohler, M. (2020). Intercultural language teaching and learning in classroom practice. In J. Jackson (Ed.), *The Routledge handbook of language and intercultural communication* (2nd ed., pp. 413–426). Routledge.

Komisarof, A., & Zhu, H. (2016). Making sense of transnational academics' experiences: Constructive marginality in liminal spaces. In A. Komisarof & H. Zhu (Eds.), *Crossing boundaries and weaving intercultural work, life, and scholarship in globalizing universities* (pp. 174–200). Routledge.

Kramsch, C. (2009). *The multilingual subject.* Oxford University Press.

Kramsch, C. (2014). Identity and subjectivity: Different timescales, different methodologies. In F. Dervin & K. Risager (Eds.), *Researching identity and interculturality* (pp. 211–230). Routledge.

Kramsch, C., & Uryu, M. (2020). Intercultural contact, hybridity and third space. In J. Jackson (Ed.), *The Routledge handbook of language and intercultural communication* (2nd ed., pp. 204–218). Routledge.

Kubota, R., & Lin, A. (Eds.). (2009). Race, culture, and identities in second language education: Exploring critically engaged practice. Routledge.

Ladegaard, H. J. (2017a). *The discourse of powerlessness and repression: Life stories of domestic migrant workers in Hong Kong*. Routledge.

Ladegaard, H. J. (2017b). The disquieting tension of "the other": University students' experience of sojourn in Hong Kong. *Journal of Multilingual and Multicultural Development, 37*(3), 268–282. https://doi.org/10.1080/01434632.2015.1134552.

Ladegaard, H. J. (2019). Reconceptualising "home", "family" and "self": Identity struggles in domestic migrant worker returnee narratives. *Language and Intercultural Communication, 19*(3), 289–303. https://doi.org/10.1080/14708477.2018.1509984.

Ladegaard, H. J. (2020). Language competence, identity construction and discursive boundary-making: Distancing and alignment in domestic migrant worker narratives. *International Journal of the Sociology of Language, 262*, 97–122. https://doi.org/10.1515/ijsl-2019-2071.

Lam, W. S. E. (2000). L2 literacy and the design of the self: A case study of a teenager writing on the internet. *TESOL Quarterly, 34*(3), 457–482.

Lam, W. S. E. (2004) Second language socialization in a bilingual chat room: Global and local considerations. *Language Learning & Technology, 8*(3), 44–66.

Lam, W. S. E., & Christiansen, M. S. (2022). Transnational Mexican youth negotiating languages, identities, and cultures online: A chronotopic lens. *TESOL Quarterly, 56*(3), 907–933.

Lam, W. S. E., & Warriner, D. S. (2012). Transnationalism and literacy: Investigating the mobility of people, languages, texts, and practices in contexts of migration. *Reading Research Quarterly, 47*(2), 191–215.

Leander, K. (2008). Toward a connective ethnography of online/offline literacy networks. In J. Coiro, M. Knobel, C. Lankshear, & D. Leu (Eds.), *Handbook of research on new literacies* (pp. 33–65). Lawrence Erlbaum.

Lee, C. (2018). Introduction: Discourse of social tagging. *Discourse, Context & Media, 22*, 1–3.

Li, W. (2011). Multilinguality, multimodality, and multicompetence: Code- and modeswitching by minority ethnic children in complementary schools. *Modern Language Journal, 95*, 370–384.

Li, W., & Zhu, H. (2013). Translanguaging identities: Creating transnational space through flexible multilingual practices amongst Chinese university students in the UK. *Applied Linguistics, 34*(5), 516–535. https://doi.org/10.1093/applin/amt022.

Lin, A. (2014). Critical discourse analysis in applied linguistics: A methodological review. *Annual Review of Applied Linguistics, 34,* 213–232.

Lin, A., Grant, R., Kubota, R., et al. (2004). Women faculty of color in TESOL: Theorizing our lived experiences. *TESOL Quarterly, 38*(3), 487–504.

Lincoln, Y. S., & Guba, E. G. (2000). Paradigmatic controversies, contradictions, and emerging confluences. In N. K. Denzin & Y. S. Lincoln (Eds.), *Handbook of qualitative research* (2nd ed., pp. 163–188). SAGE.

Lockwood, J. (2015). Virtual team management: What is causing communication breakdown? *Language and Intercultural Communication, 15*(1), 125–140. https://doi.org/10.1080/14708477.2014.985310.

MacMaster, N. (2001). *Racism in Europe.* Palgrave.

Makoni, S., & Pennycook, A. (Eds.). (2007). *Disinventing and reconstituting languages* (Vol. 62). Multilingual Matters.

Marra, M., & Holmes, J. (2007). Humour across cultures: Joking in the multicultural workplace. In H. Kotthoff & H. Spencer-Oatey (Eds.), *Handbook of intercultural communication* (pp. 153–172). Mouton de Gruyter.

Martin, J. N., & Nakayama, T. K. (2015). Reconsidering intercultural (communication) competence in the workplace: A dialectical approach. *Language and Intercultural Communication, 15*(1), 13–28. https://doi.org/10.1080/14708477.2014.985303.

McKinney, C. (2007). "If I speak English does it make me less black anyway?" "Race" and English in South African desegregated schools. *English Academy Review, 24*(2), 6–24.

Mercer, S. (2011). *Towards an understanding of language learner self-concept.* Springer.

Mitchell, R., Tracy-Ventura, N., & McManus, K. (Eds.). (2015). *Social interaction, identity and language learning during residence abroad.* European Second Language Association.

Mitchell, R., Tracy-Ventura, N., & McManus, K. (2017). *Anglophone students abroad: Identity, social relationships, and language learning.* Routledge.

Miyahara, M. (2015). *Emerging self-identities and emotion in foreign language learning: A narrative-oriented approach.* Multilingual Matters.

Moody, S. J. (2019). Contextualizing macro-level identities and constructing inclusiveness through teasing and self-mockery: A view from the intercultural workplace in Japan. *Journal of Pragmatics, 152,* 145–159. https://doi.org/10.1016/j.pragma.2019.05.023.

Motha, S. (2006). Racializing ESOL teacher identities in US K12 public schools. *TESOL Quarterly, 40*(3), 495–518.

Motha, S. (2020). Is an antiracist and decolonizing applied linguistics possible? *Annual Review of Applied Linguistics, 40,* 128–133.

Nevile, M., & Wagner, J. (2011). Language choice and participation: Two practices for switching languages in institutional interaction. In G. Pallotti & J. Wagner (Eds.), *L2 learning as social practice: Conversation-analytic perspectives* (pp. 211–235). University of Hawai'i.

Norton, B. (2000). *Identity and language learning: Gender, ethnicity and educational change.* Longman Pearson Education.

Norton, B. (2013). *Identity and language learning: Extending the conversation* (2nd ed.). Multilingual Matters.

Norton, B., & Early, M. (2011). Researcher identity, narrative inquiry, and language teaching research. *TESOL Quarterly, 45,* 415–439.

Norton, B., & Pavlenko, A. (2019). Imagined communities, identity, and English language learning in a multilingual world. In X. Gao (Ed.), *Second handbook of English language teaching* (pp. 703–718). Springer.

Norton Peirce, B. (1995). Social identity, investment, and language learning. *TESOL Quarterly, 29*(1), 9–31.

Papacharissi, Z. (Ed.). (2010). *A networked self: Identity, community, and culture on social network sites.* Routledge.

Pavlenko, A. (2002a). Poststructuralist approaches to the study of social factors in second language learning and use. In V. Cook (Ed.), *Portraits of the L2 user* (pp. 277–302). Multilingual Matters.

Pavlenko, A. (2002b). Narrative study: Whose story is it, anyway? *TESOL Quarterly, 36,* 213–218.

Pavlenko, A. (2007). Autobiographic narratives as data in applied linguistics. *Applied Linguistics, 28,* 163–188.

Pavlenko, A., & Blackledge, A. (Eds.). (2004). *Negotiation of identities in multilingual contexts.* Multilingual Matters.

Pennycook, A. (2007). *Global Englishes and transcultural flows.* Routledge.

Piller, I. (2017). *Intercultural communication: A critical introduction* (2nd ed.). Edinburgh University Press.

Puri, J. (2004). *Encountering nationalism.* Blackwell.

Rampton, B. (2017). *Crossing: Language and ethnicity among adolescents.* Routledge.

Risager, K. (2006). *Language and culture: Global flows and local complexity.* Multilingual Matters.

Rudolph, N. (2023). Narratives and negotiations of identity in Japan and critical-ity in (English) language education:(Dis) connections and implications. *TESOL Quarterly, 57*(2), 375–401.

Schecter, S. R., & Bayley, R. (1997). Language socialization practices and cultural identity: Case studies of Mexican-descent families in California and Texas. *TESOL Quarterly, 31*(3), 513–541. https://doi.org/10.2307/3587836.

Shi, X., Chang, Y., & Gao, J. (2022). Investment in transnational identity to become microcelebrities in China: On American uploaders' success in a Chinese video-sharing website. *Language and Intercultural Communication, 22*(6), 1–20. https://doi.org/10.1080/14708477.2022.2078343.

Shuck, G. (2006). Racializing the nonnative English speaker. *Journal of Language, Identity and Education, 5*(4), 259–276.

Song, J. (2010). Language ideology and identity in transnational space: Globalization, migration, and bilingualism among Korean families in the USA. *International Journal of Bilingual Education and Bilingualism, 13*(1), 23–42. https://doi.org/10.1080/13670050902748778.

Spivak, G. (1996). Subaltern studies: Deconstructing historiography? In D. Landry & G. MacLean (Eds.), *The Spivak reader* (pp. 203–237). Routledge.

Steinhardt, H. C., Li, L. C., & Jiang, Y. (2018). The identity shift in Hong Kong since 1997: Measurement and explanation. *Journal of Contemporary China, 27*(110), 261–276.

Stornaiuolo, A., Hull, G., & Nelson, M. E. (2009). Mobile texts and migrant audiences: Rethinking literacy and assessment in a new media age. *Language Arts, 86*(5), 382–392.

Sue, D. W. (2003). *Overcoming our racism: The journey to liberation.* John Wiley & Sons.

Sun, T. (2020). *Second language identities and socialization during study abroad: Chinese STEM international exchange students in an English-speaking country* (UMI No. 28960501) [Doctoral dissertation, The Chinese University of Hong Kong]. ProQuest Dissertations and Theses Global.

Tajfel, H. (1982). Social psychology of intergroup relations. *Annual Review of Psychology, 33*, 1–39.

Talmy, S. (2009). Resisting ESL: Categories and sequence in a critically "motivated" analysis of classroom interaction. In H. Nguyen & G. Kasper (Eds.), *Talk-in interaction: Multilingual perspectives* (pp. 181–213). University of Hawai'i.

Thorne, S. L. (2016). Cultures-of-use and morphologies of communicative action. *Language Learning and Technology, 20*(2), 185–191.

Thorne, S. L., & Black, R. W. (2011). Identity and interaction in Internet-mediated contexts. In C. Higgins (Ed.), *Identity formation in globalizing contexts: Language learning in the new millennium* (pp. 257–278). de Gruyter.

Tupas, R. (Ed.). (2015). *Unequal Englishes: The politics of Englishes today.* Springer.

Tupas, R. (2019). Entanglements of colonialism, social class, and *Unequal Englishes. Journal of Sociolinguistics, 23*(5), 529–542.

Van Dijck, J., Poell, T., & de Waal, M. (2018). *The platform society: Public values in a connective world.* Oxford University Press.

Wacquant, L. (2003). Ethnografeast: A progress report on the practice and promise of ethnography. *Ethnography, 4*(1), 5–14.

Weedon, C. (1987). *Feminist practice and poststructuralist theory.* Basil Blackwell.

Weedon, C. (2004). *Identity and culture: Narratives of difference and belonging.* Open University Press.

Wenger, E. (1998). *Communities of practice: Learning, meaning, and identity.* Cambridge University Press.

Whitworth, K. F. (2006). Access to language learning during study abroad: The roles of identity and subject positioning (UMI No. 3229461) [Doctoral dissertation, The Pennsylvania State University]. ProQuest Dissertations and Theses Global.

Wodak, R. (Ed.). (1997). *Gender and discourse.* SAGE.

Wolcott, H. (2008). *Ethnography: A way of seeing.* Altamira Press.

Zhu, H. (2014). *Exploring intercultural communication: Language in action.* Routlodgc.

Zhu, H. (2019). *Exploring intercultural communication: Language in action* (2nd ed.). Abingdon: Routledge.

Zhu, H., & Li, W. (2016). Transnational experience, aspiration and family language policy. *Journal of Multilingual and Multicultural Development, 37*(7), 655–666. https://doi.org/10.1080/01434632.2015.1127928.

Zhu, H., & Li, W. (2020). Translanguaging, identity, and migration. In J. Jackson (Ed.), *The Routledge handbook of language and intercultural communication* (2nd ed., pp. 234–248). Routledge.

Zotzmann, K., & O'Regan, J. (2016). Critical discourse analysis and identity. In S. Preece (Ed.), *Routledge handbook of language and identity* (pp. 113–127). Routledge.

About the Authors

Ron Darvin is an Assistant Professor at the Department of Language and Literacy Education of the University of British Columbia in Vancouver, Canada. His research examines issues of identity and investment in language learning, technology, and critical pedagogy. He has published in the *Annual Review of Applied Linguistics, Language Teaching* and *Language and Intercultural Communication*, and is the recipient of the 2020 Dissertation Award of the American Association of Applied Linguistics (AAAL), and the 2017 Emerging Scholar Award of the American Educational Research Association (AERA) Language and Social Processes SIG.

Tongle Sun is a Lecturer in the Department of English at The Chinese University of Hong Kong, where she is teaching undergraduate and postgraduate courses in applied English linguistics. Her research interests are language, culture, and identity, language socialization, study abroad, intercultural communication, and English for specific purposes.

Intercultural Communication

Will Baker

University of Southampton

Will Baker is Director of the Centre for Global Englishes and an Associate Professor of Applied Linguistics, University of Southampton. His research interests are Intercultural and Transcultural Communication, English as a Lingua Franca, English medium education, Intercultural education and ELT, and he has published and presented internationally in all these areas. Recent publications include: *Intercultural and Transcultural Awareness in Language Teaching* (2022), co-author of *Transcultural Communication through Global Englishes* (2021), co-editor of *The Routledge Handbook of English as a Lingua Franca* (2018). He is also co-editor of the book series 'Developments in English as Lingua Franca'.

Troy McConachy

University of Warwick

Troy McConachy is Associate Professor in Applied Linguistics at the University of Warwick. His work aims to make interdisciplinary connections between the fields of language education, intercultural communication, and social psychology, focusing particularly on the role of metapragmatic awareness in intercultural communication and intercultural learning. He is author of *Developing Intercultural Perspectives on Language Use: Exploring Pragmatics and Culture in Foreign Language Learning (2018)*, Editor-in-Chief of the international journal *Intercultural Communication Education*, and co-editor of *Teaching and Learning Second Language Pragmatics for Intercultural Understanding* and *Intercultural Learning and Language Education and Beyond: Evolving Concepts, Perspectives and Practices.*

Sonia Morán Panero

University of Southampton

Sonia Morán Panero is a Lecturer in Applied Linguistics at the University of Southampton. Her academic expertise is on the sociolinguistics of the use and learning of English for transcultural communication purposes. Her work has focused particularly on language ideologies around Spanish and English as global languages, English language policies and education in Spanish-speaking settings and English medium instruction on global education. She has published on these areas through international knowledge dissemination platforms such as ELTJ, JELF, *The Routledge Handbook of English as a Lingua Franca* (2018) and the British Council.

About the Series

This series offers a mixture of key texts and innovative research publications from established and emerging scholars which represent the depth and diversity of current intercultural communication research and suggest new directions for the field.

Cambridge Elements ≡

Intercultural Communication

Elements in the Series